PagePlus X3 User Guide

How to Contact Us

**Our main office
(UK, Europe):**

The Software Centre
PO Box 2000, Nottingham,
NG11 7GW, UK

Main:	(0115) 914 2000
Registration (UK only):	(0800) 376 1989
Sales (UK only):	(0800) 376 7070
Customer Service/ Technical Support:	http://www.serif.com/support
General Fax:	(0115) 914 2020

**North American office
(USA, Canada):**

The Software Center
13 Columbia Drive, Suite 5, Amherst
NH 03031, USA

Main:	(603) 889-8650
Registration:	(800) 794-6876
Sales:	(800) 55-SERIF or 557-3743
Customer Service/ Technical Support:	http://www.serif.com/support
General Fax:	(603) 889-1127

Online

Visit us on the Web at: http://www.serif.com/

International

Please contact your local distributor/dealer. For further details, please contact us at one of our phone numbers above.

Contents

1. Welcome 1
   Welcome! 3
   Installation 11

2. Getting Started 17
   Startup Wizard 19
   Creating a publication from a design template 20
   Starting a new publication from scratch 20
   Opening an existing publication 21
   Importing PagePlus documents 22
   Importing PDF files 22
   Working with more than one publication 23
   Saving your publication 24
   Closing the publication 24
   Updating and saving defaults 24

3. Working with Pages 27
   Setting up a publication 29
   Understanding master pages 31
   Viewing pages 32
   Navigating 34
   Adding, removing, and rearranging pages 35
   Working with layers 36
   Setting guides for page margins, rows, columns, and bleeds 42
   Using the rulers and dot grid 44
   Using headers and footers 48
   Using page numbering 48

4. Working with Objects 51

Selecting an object..53
Selecting multiple objects 54
Snapping..55
Creating groups 56
Copying, pasting, and replicating objects..........................56
Moving objects 59
Resizing objects 59
Locking an object's size or position...................................60
Ordering objects...60
Aligning and distributing objects 61
Exporting as a picture 62
Rotating an object...64
Flipping an object...65
Cropping and combining objects.......................................65
Adding borders...69
Hyperlinking an object..70

5. Working with Text... 73

Importing text from a file 75
Understanding text frames...75
Fitting text to frames 81
Linking text frames...83
Using artistic text...85
Creating logos..87
Putting text on a path 90
Editing text on the page 92
Using Find and Replace...96
Inserting footnotes and endnotes......................................97
Setting text properties 97
Using fonts 98
Substituting fonts 100
Using text styles..104

Wrapping text 109

Creating a bulleted or numbered list 111

Inserting a symbol 115

Inserting date/time 116

Inserting user details 116

Viewing and changing document information 117

Using AutoCorrect and AutoSpell 118

Spell-checking 119

Automatic proofreading 120

Using the thesaurus 121

Creating text-based tables 122

Manipulating tables 123

Using QuickClear and QuickFill 128

Formatting numbers 129

Inserting formulas 129

Inserting a calendar 130

Inserting database tables 133

Creating a table of contents 135

Creating an index 136

Producing a book with BookPlus 137

Using mail merge 141

Checking fonts and resources used 142

6. Images, Lines, and Shapes 145

Importing pictures 147

Adding picture frames 150

Using the Media Bar 152

Using the Gallery 156

Importing TWAIN images 158

Using the Image Cutout Studio 160

Drawing and editing lines 163

Setting line properties 167

Drawing and editing shapes 169

Applying 2D filter effects 172
Using 3D filter effects...175
Applying a mesh warp envelope 178
Adding dimensionality (Instant 3D) 179
Using object styles 181
Using connectors 184

7. Colour, Fills, and Transparency 187

Applying solid fills...189
Working with gradient and bitmap fills................................190
Using schemes 193
Managing publication palettes 196
Working with transparency...199

8. Printing your Publication 201

Printing basics..203
Previewing the printed page 204
Printing special formats..205
Generating professional output 207
Manual duplex printing 208
Saving print profiles 209

9. Publishing and Sharing 211

Exporting PDF files 213
Creating a PDF bookmark list 214
Creating a PDF slideshow 216
Sharing by email 218

10. Using PDF Forms 221

Getting started with PDF forms 223
Creating PDF forms 225
Collecting data from forms 228

11. Producing Web Pages 233

Getting started in Web mode 235
Viewing hyperlinks in your publication 236
Adding hotspots 236
Web site colours 238
Setting Web picture display options 240
Choosing Web page properties.................................... 241
Adding animation effects.. 241
Adding sound and video... 242
Adding Java applets.. 243
Publishing a Web site to a local folder 244
Previewing your Web site in a browser 244
Publishing to the Web 245
Maintaining your Web site.. 247

12. Index..249

Welcome

Welcome!

Welcome to PagePlus X4, the award-winning Desktop Publishing solution! Fully certified for Windows Vista, PagePlus is the easiest way to get stunning publishing results, whether you're a home or business user. For anyone from home to corporate publisher, to design their designs as outstanding printed documents, Acrobat PDFs, PDF slideshows, even HTML web sites and eye-catching e-books.

If you've purchased PagePlus to explore for the first time, you've made a great choice! We're sure you'll soon be producing impressive documents with both speed and simplicity. For experienced users, PagePlus X4 offers additional performance enhances.

What's New?

- **Quick-and-easy Cut-Out (group p. 150)**
  Image Cutout Studio really lights up work of cutting out your placed images, directly in PagePlus. Use brush-to discard unwanted or to photo tidies up. It's easy to keep subjects of interest (people, objects, etc.) a files, or delete unwanted background or feathering to impart an airy profile, or well-defined cutout edges to seamlessly merge your cutout into your page design.

- **Stunning logos with Logostudio (new...)**
  Create your own logos in an integrated LogoStudio environment, dedicated to professional high-quality design. Start with a preset design then customize, or base your own design on existing PagePlus objects... either way you'll get professional logos to use across private branding that will impress even your important clients.

- **Manual Duplex printing (p. ...)**
  For use on printers without duplex support, use the "manual duplex" wizard to create any double-sided publication. Simply follow on-screen printable instructions and flip your paper when prompted!

- **Import PDF Photos and Text (group p. ...)**
  Import Microsoft Word, PDF, Photo, HTML, or any text... with the new PDF and Text importer to work PagePlus. Opening an electronic document, making changes and saving as PagePlus or web document. Import and manipulate from all the major PDF versions with flexible output.

- **Black-and-white ...**
  Convert color documents to grayscale for printing black-and-white or with a limited color palette in a publication file makes PagePlus ideal for newsletters and price lists. New controls let you choose in... and preview your publication in black-and-white.

Welcome!

Welcome to **PagePlus X3**, the award-winning Desktop Publishing solution fully certified for Windows Vista. PagePlus is the easiest way to get superior publishing results, whether on your desktop or via professional printing. It's simple for anyone to create, publish and share their designs as outstanding printed documents, stunning PDFs, PDF slideshows, stylish Web sites and eye-catching emails.

If you've upgraded from a previous version, this new edition of PagePlus includes a host of **exciting new features** which keeps PagePlus ahead of its competitors and at a fraction of the price! We hope you also enjoy the additional power and performance edge.

What's New?

- **Quick-and-easy Image Cutouts** (p. 160)
  Image Cutout Studio makes light work of cutting out your placed images, directly in PagePlus. Use brushes to discard uniform backgrounds (sky, walls, etc.) or keep subjects of interest (people, objects, etc.). Use an advanced transparency blending or feathering technique at a poorly- or well-defined cutout edge to seamlessly merge your cutout into your page design.

- **Stunning logos with LogoStudio** (p. 87)
  Create striking logos in an integrated Studio environment with a major focus on detailed high-quality design. Start with one of a range of **Logo templates** or base your logo on existing PagePlus objects—either way lets you create vector-based logos for corporate or private branding that will make a strong impact on your clientele. Equally great for publications or Web site banners!

- **Manual Duplex printing** (p. 208)
  For desktop printers without duplex support, use the **Manual Duplex Wizard** to create any double-sided publication. Simply follow on-screen or printable instructions and flip your paper when prompted!

- **Import HD Photos and PostScript files** (p. 147)
  Import Microsoft's new **HD Photo** High-Definition images as well as Encapsulated PostScript files (.EPS); display previews avoid unnecessary rendering and redraw of PostScript graphics. All the latest RAW formats from all the major digital camera manufacturers are supported.

- **Package your project**
  Gather together your project's supporting files to allow your project to be used on a different computer or at a print bureau. Resources such as fonts, linked graphics, linked media files, and more, are embedded in a project **package**—you'll never suffer from missing resources again!

- **Feather for cropped objects** (p. 66)
  Feather your square or irregular crop outline to soften a cropped object's edge. Great for creating vignetting on wedding photos, and more.

- **New stunning Filter Effects** (p. 172 and 175)
  Make reflections of an object—great for logos, icons, and image content! **Blur** any object or stroke a coloured solid or gradient **outline** around object edges (use the new Contour fill which applies gradient fill from the inner to outer outline width). **3D effects** are boosted with **Reflection Maps** which offer a realistic glass-like **transparency** control of non-reflective/reflective surfaces. Multiple separately coloured lights are added for dramatic **lighting effects**. All filter effects can now be applied in preview mode or to the object on the page.

- **Shared frame and artistic text properties** (p. 73)
  Apply gradient colour fills and transparency to **table** and **frame text**, as for artistic text; apply to selected characters, whole words or even entire paragraphs!

- **Control Text Fitting in Frames and Text paths** (p. 81)
  Use **Fit Text**, **Enlarge Text**, and **Shrink Text** to control how text fits in a single or linked frames. Switch on/off **Autofit** or **Shrink text on Overflow** on a per frame basis. **Text paths** also now benefit from improved text fitting.

- **Table enhancements** (p. 123)
  Adopt absolute cell references using the $ notation seen in popular spreadsheet programs (e.g., A2). Add/remove columns/rows by dragging end headers. Use in-context drop-down menus on row/column headers to drag out new rows or columns. Benefit from resizing of table columns without affecting overall table width.

- **A New Metafile Format** (p. 147)
  Import and Export **Serif Metafiles** (.SMF), a proprietary image format with improvements to the Windows Metafile format (WMF). Better line, fill, and text definitions make them ideal for sharing graphics between Serif applications.

- **Customized keyboard shortcuts and toolbars**
  Take advantage of customizable keyboard shortcuts—assign your own keystrokes to toolbar and menu commands, even to text styles! Tailor PagePlus to your needs with user-friendly toolbar and icon customization. Drag and drop options onto your own bespoke toolbar.

..and some great new enhancements!

Hyperlink to anchors attached to text, shapes, or images. Rotate objects about a moveable on-the-page origin point. Preserve original arrows shapes and curved corners by **locking QuickShape geometry**. **Import multiple pictures** and paste one by one! Swap the User Interface look-and-feel—choose Silver, Blue, Aqua, Silver-Blue, or Classic. Support for Word 2007 text import filter. The **Styles tab** gets a completely new look, with an **Object Styles Manager** for creating new or rearranging categories. Define your own **pasteboard colours**! Drawn **ruler guides** can now adopt different colours (even the current layer's colour). For Web publishing, **colour schemes** now offer an off-page browser window **Background colour** and **On-page colour** settings. Additionally, the Web page **Layout Checker** has been improved

Key features

Before you get started with PagePlus, we recommend you take the opportunity
to familiarize yourself with PagePlus key features and capabilities.

Layout

- **Versatile Setup with Auto-Imposition**
  Just click to specify layouts for small (business cards and labels), folded
  (booklets and greetings cards), and large publications (banners and posters)!

- **Ready-to-go Design Templates**
  Fancy a quick route to produce stunning designs for home or business use?
  Adopt one of an impressive collection of eye-catching **Design Templates**.

- **Master Pages**
  Save time and maintain consistency by using multiple master pages assigned
  to your publication pages.

- **Layers**
  Each page can have multiple layers—so you can assign elements to different
  layers for modular design.

- **Professional layout tools**
  Movable **rulers**, **guide lines** and a **dot grid**, as layout aids, help you finely
  position objects; snapping jumps an object to guide or grid. Use **Sticky
  guides**, a great way of moving (in bulk) all objects snapped to your guide
  lines—move the guide and objects will follow!

- **Page control**
  Add and **remove pages** in just a few clicks of your mouse in the **Pages tab**.
  Even drag and drop pages within the tab to reorder sequence. Assign master
  pages to several document pages at once. To view pages, **Multi-page view**
  lets you see an array of pages, even show a facing pages view!

- **Mail & Photo Merge**
  With Mail and Photo Merge, read data from just about any source: tables
  from HTML Web pages, database files, even live ODBC servers! Print to
  labels and letters equally.

- **Tables and Calendars**
  Choose from a range of preset formats or design your own table. Use the
  convenient Table context toolbar to sort data, format cells, and choose from
  a wide range of functions for **spreadsheet calculations** (use absolute cell
  references). **Calendars** are table-based for enhanced functionality, and
  support Year update, inline personal events, and public holidays!

- **BookPlus**
  Treat separate PagePlus publication files as chapters and use the **BookPlus** utility to link them into a book! Assign text styles and colour palettes across publications, automatically generate an Index or Table of Contents, add page numbering and output your final long document to both print and PDF.

Graphics

- **Import Pictures**
  Import commonly-used standard file formats, including all the latest RAW digital camera formats. **AutoFlow** pictures (or drag and drop) from the always-at-hand **Media Bar** into sequential shaped **picture frames**! Import Photoshop files directly into your PagePlus publications.

- **Image Adjustments**
  Apply **adjustments** (Brightness & Contrast, fix red eye, and many more) and **enhancements** (Diffuse Glow, Dust and Scratch Remover). For advanced image manipulation use **Edit in PhotoPlus**, which accesses Serif's award-winning photo-editing package (if installed).

- **Drawing Tools**
  Design stunning vector graphics with Pencil, Pen and Straight **Line tools**. Alternatively, the array of fully-customizable **QuickShapes** let you quickly create outlines for your designs, while **Convert to Curves**, **Crop to Shape**, Curve drawing and Warp tools offer complete flexibility for creating any shape imaginable! Apply **line styles** to all kinds of shapes—even add line endings like arrowheads and diamonds. **Mesh warp envelopes** add perspective, slant, and bulge to any object.

- **Fills**
  Enhance shapes and artistic text with fantastic professional fills. Use the **Colour tab** to change fill, line, or text colour with one click. Choose preset fills (solid, gradient, or bitmap) from the **Swatches tab's** palettes—even create stunning bitmap fills from your own images. What's more, every colour used is added to the **Publication Palette** so that you can easily re-use it again and again.

- **Intelligent Colour Schemes**
  Choose from dozens of preset **colour schemes** to change the overall appearance of your publications with a single click. You can customize the scheme colours, create brand new schemes, and apply any scheme to a "from-scratch" publication.

- **Ready-to-go Styles**
  Choose various filter effects, glows, shadows, textures, and materials from the **Styles tab**. Customize the preset styles or store your own!

- **Transparency**
  Add transparency to your backgrounds, text frames, tables, shapes and text to achieve a truly professional look. As with colour fills, you can apply **solid**, **gradient**, and **bitmap** transparencies—even create bitmap transparencies from your own image collection.

- **Filter Effects**
  Apply eye-catching **Filter Effects** to make your images and text really stand out. Easily add shadows, glows, bevels, blurs, reflections, outlines, feathering, or embossing effects and alter the flexible settings for exactly the right look—your original object remains intact and editable if you change your mind! Use the **Shadow Tool** for on the page control of basic or skewed drop shadows.

- **Astounding 3D Lighting and Surface Effects**
  Advanced algorithms **bring flat shapes to life**! Choose one or more effects, then vary surface and source light properties. Start with a pattern or a function, adjust parameters for incredible surface contours, textures, fills—realistic-looking wood, water, skin, marble and much more.

- **Instant 3D**
  Transform your artistic text and shapes into impressive 3D objects directly on the page! Apply multiple coloured **lighting effects** (with directional control), along with custom **bevel** and **lathe** effect profiles to create your very own unique contours.

- **Connector Tools**
  Easily design organizational charts, family trees and other diagrams—connectors will link your boxes, circles, or other shapes together, with links being maintained during any object repositioning.

Text

- **Text Frames**
  Compose story text in **text frames** then easily position, rotate or size the frame to suit; connected frames host the same story text and can be filled automatically by **AutoFlow**. Intelligently control how text fits to frames. Enhanced **text wrap options** and separate crop and wrap outlines mean you have greater control over where text flows and how it appears. Import, paste, export text in **Unicode** format... design with a foreign-language or special fonts and characters.

- **Text Control**
  Apply text formatting from an on-hand text context toolbar; apply **multi-level bullet and numbering schemas** to your paragraphs, even to your text styles; a **Text Styles tab** for allocating text attributes to chosen paragraphs; flexible bullet, numbering and indenting buttons; and much more!

- **Fonts**
  Substitute missing fonts when opening third-party publications. View your currently installed font set in the **Fonts tab**, including those most recently assigned to text, favourite fonts, and those considered WebSafe. Hover over a listed font for an "in-situ" **font preview** of your selected text—simply click to apply the new font if you like it! Easily **swap** all selected instances of a common font for another font in one fell swoop!

- **Frame and Artistic Text**
  Create text with stunning transparency effects, gradient/bitmap (photo) fills, 2D/3D effects and more. Use designer **artistic text** for high impact headlines and powerful design elements— artistic text scales, flips, and can follow a drawn path, while **frame text** flows and line wraps.

- **Multilingual Support**
  Create **multiple-language** documents in PagePlus. You can mark words, paragraphs or whole stories with a language and PagePlus will automatically check the spelling for you in that language.

- **Find & Replace**
  Search through story text for words and phrases but also text attributes, particular fonts, colours, special characters (Unicode), regular expressions, and words at specific positions in sentences.

- **Text Composition Tools**
  Includes word count, spell-checking, thesaurus, and proof reader. **AutoCorrect** and **AutoSpell** proofing options are at hand.

- **Table of Contents & Index**
  Create automated **Tables of Contents** and **Indexes** for complex documents. PagePlus refers to the named styles you've allocated to headings, subheadings and titles to automatically create your Table of Contents, with up to six levels. Indexing documents is simple too, use the intuitive tools to select important terms and let PagePlus do the rest.

Publishing

- **PDF Import & Export**
  Import PDF documents as new PagePlus publications or **insert a PDF document's contents** into existing publications. Either way, PDF contents can be easily edited within PagePlus—the text and paragraph formatting of the original PDF document is maintained. Export your documents to PDF, with powerful options to publish your PDFs for professional printing (PDF/X) and the Web (streaming supported).

- **PDF Forms**
  Create your own electronic **PDF form**, requesting information from form recipients. Your recipients can type in their responses, then save, print or submit their form electronically. Serif will email you completed forms, or you can set up your own Web submission service.

- **PDF Slideshows**
  Create attention-grabbing **PDF slideshows** with stylish page and layer transitions —even add sound and video clips! Share with friends, family, and colleagues.

- **ICC Colour Profiling**
  Set up ICC (International Colour Consortium) profiles for your monitor, printer and scanner, and be confident that your printed colours will closely match their appearance on-screen. Avoid wasting time, paper and ink!

- **Printing**
  Print documents professionally on your home printer—as several pages on one sheet, or for large format printing, a single page across multiple sheets.

- **Email Publications**
  Share your PagePlus documents as graphically-rich HTML emails, complete with text, images, and active hyperlinks visible in the body of the email.

- **Publish To Web**
  Design your own Web site directly in PagePlus or publish pages originally created for print to the web as well. PagePlus's intuitive Web Publishing mode creates all the background HTML code for you and guides you seamlessly through publishing your documents and Web sites online (either in full or incrementally).

Don't forget to register your new copy, using the **Registration Wizard**, also on the Help menu. That way, we can keep you informed of new developments and future upgrades!

Installation

System Requirements

Minimum:

- Pentium PC with DVD/CD drive and mouse

- Microsoft Windows® 2000, XP or Vista operating system

- 256MB RAM

- 408MB free hard disk space (1.22GB with Resource DVD installed)

- SVGA display (800x600 resolution, 16-bit colour) display or higher

Additional disk resources and memory are required when editing large and/or complex documents.

Optional:

- Windows-compatible printer

- TWAIN-compatible scanner and/or digital camera

- Stylus or other input device

- 3D Accelerated graphics card with DirectX 9 (or above) or OpenGL support

- Internet account and connection required for Web Publishing features and accessing online resources

First-time install

To install Serif PagePlus X3, simply insert the Program CD into your DVD/CD drive. If AutoPlay is enabled on the drive, this automatically starts the Setup Wizard. If you are installing PagePlus on Microsoft Windows® Vista, you may need to click on **Run autorun.exe** from within the **Autoplay** dialog. If AutoPlay is not enabled (or doesn't start the install automatically), use the Manual install method described below.

The Setup Wizard begins with a Welcome dialog, click **Next**. Follow the steps of the wizard, clicking **Next** each time to proceed. At this point, you may be informed that there is a reboot pending. If this happens, we recommend rebooting your PC. Remember to remove the Program CD from the drive and to close all other applications before you restart. The Setup Wizard should now run successfully when the CD is replaced in the DVD/CD drive.

Please read through the licence agreement. Click **Next**.

Enter your User Name, Organization (if applicable) and the software **Product Key** that came with your software (on your CD's case).

For more information, click the ⌨ button. Click **Next**. Proceed through the following dialogs making appropriate choices as per your requirements.

At the **Setup Options** dialog, you have the opportunity to customize your installation.

To install the recommended options, simply click **Next**. However, if you are concerned about disk space, you may choose to run some of the features from the DVD/CD. The drop-down boxes display the available options for each feature:

- ▭ **Will be installed on the local hard drive.** If this option is selected, it will install the feature to your hard disk but will not automatically install any subfeatures that may be available.

- ▭▤ **Entire feature will be installed on the local hard drive.** By selecting this option, all of the subfeatures relating to this feature will also be installed. Some subfeatures can require a substantial amount of hard disk space.

- ⊗ **Will be installed to run from the CD.** If this option is selected, you will save space on your hard disk but you will need to have the installation media at hand to access the features.

- ⊗▤ **Entire feature will be installed to run from the CD**. This option will allow you to access the content and all of its subfeatures from the installation media, saving you disk space.

- 🖬 **Will be installed to run from network.** If you are installing the software from a network, this option will allow you to access the content from the network storage, saving you disk space.

- 🖬▤ **Entire feature will be installed to run from network.** If you are installing the software from a network, this option will allow you to access the features and all related subfeatures from the network storage, saving you disk space.

- ✗ **Entire feature will be unavailable.** By choosing this option, you will not be able to use the selected feature. However, if you later decide that you want to use the feature, you will be able to install it by modifying your installation.

When you select a feature installation option, the information pane on the right of the list will inform you of the amount of hard disk space that the feature needs. Not all installation options are available for all features.

> If disk space is not an issue, you may decide to install the entire program to your hard disk. This can improve performance and you will be able to use all of the features without the need to keep the program disk in your DVD/CD drive.

If you do not want to install the program to its default location, click the **Change** button. Browse to the folder that you want to install PagePlus in and click **OK**. Caution should be taken here as changing the default settings may affect subsequent installs of later versions of the software.

> CAUTION: Changing the installation defaults may result in some options of the program being unavailable. It is only recommended for advanced users.

At the Shortcut Options screen, you can choose to automatically create shortcuts by checking the option boxes. Click **Next.**

Click **Install** to accept your settings and install the program. The dialog will display a progress bar as the program installs. Once installation is complete, click **Finish** to exit the Setup Wizard.

(Optional) If you've also obtained the PagePlus X3 Resource DVD, install it now following the same procedure you used for the Program CD.

Your installation is now complete and you can begin using Serif PagePlus X3!

Manual install

For manual installation, use My Computer (Windows® XP), or Computer (Windows® Vista), to navigate to the DVD/CD drive in which your PagePlus Program CD is located. Double-click the DVD/CD drive and then double-click setup.exe in the displayed folder. If you are installing on Windows® Vista, choose Serif PagePlus X3 from the warning dialog (optional). Follow the on-screen installation instructions.

Modifying, Repairing or Removing PagePlus

To modify, repair or remove the installation:

Microsoft Windows® XP:

1. Click the [start] button and select **Control Panel** from the Windows Start menu.

2. Double-click on the **Add/Remove Programs** icon.

3. Locate Serif PagePlus X3 in the list of installed programs, then select it.

4. Click the **Change** button to make changes to the install via the Setup Wizard.

Microsoft Windows® Vista:

1. Click the [ ] **Start** button and click **Computer**.

2. Click the [Uninstall or change a program] button.

3. Locate Serif PagePlus X3 in the list of installed programs, then select it.

4. Click the **Change** button to make changes to the install via the Setup Wizard.

You can also access this via Programs and Features by clicking **Control Panel** from the Windows **Start** menu (or **Settings>Control Panel** from the "Classic" Windows **Start** menu), clicking **Programs** and then clicking **Programs and Features**.

To change the installed features:

Open the Setup Wizard as described in the previous steps. To change the installation, select the **Modify** option and then click **Next**. From here, you will be able to make changes such as removing some of the program features. Adding additional content may prompt you to insert your original PagePlus X3 Program CD; removing content may or may not require the CD. See the steps in **First-time install** if you are unsure about any of the options.

> Some features, such as fonts, cannot be removed by the Setup Wizard once they have been installed. This is due to the way they are used by other applications. Modifying the installation settings in this case will never free up disk space. Fonts in particular, will even remain if the program is completely uninstalled.

Removing PagePlus

Open the Setup Wizard. Select the **Remove** option and click **Next**. Click **Remove** to completely remove PagePlus from your computer.

Repairing PagePlus

On occasion, it may be necessary to repair your installation of PagePlus. This can happen if system files are overwritten by another program or if they are accidentally deleted.

Open the Setup Wizard and select the **Repair** option and click **Next**. Click **Repair**. The repair process will reinstall all files and registry entries, therefore replacing any missing or incorrectly overwritten files. Once the repair has completed, open PagePlus.

Getting Started

Startup Wizard

Once PagePlus has been installed, you're ready to start. Setup adds a **Serif PagePlus X3** item to the **(All) Programs** submenu of the Windows **Start** menu.

- Use the Windows **Start** button to pop up the Start Menu, click on **All Programs**, and then click the PagePlus item (or if PagePlus is already running, choose **New>New from Startup Wizard...** from the **File** menu).

The Startup Wizard presents the following choices:

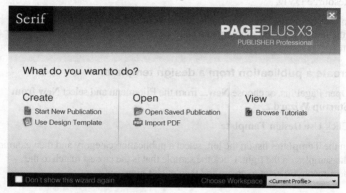

- **Start New Publication**, to open a blank page to work on.

- **Use Design Template**, to create an instant document from a pre-designed template.

- **Open Saved Publication**, to edit a saved PagePlus file.

- **Import PDF**, to create a publication from an existing PDF.

- **Browse Tutorials**, to see easy-to-follow step-by-step tutorials.

Use the **Choose Workspace** drop-down menu to choose your workspace appearance (i.e., Studio tab positions, tab sizes, and show/hide tab status). You can adopt the default workspace profile **<Default Profile>**, the last used profile **<Current Profile>**, a range of profile presets, or a workspace profile you have previously saved.

The Startup Wizard is displayed by default when you launch PagePlus. If you don't want to use the Startup Wizard again, check the "Don't show this wizard again" box. However, we suggest you leave it unchecked until you're familiar with the equivalent PagePlus commands. You can switch it on again via the **Use startup wizard** check box in **Tools>Options...** (use General menu option).

You can also access the Startup Wizard at any time from **New>New from Startup Wizard...** on the File menu.

Creating a publication from a design template

PagePlus comes complete with a whole range of categorized design templates which will speed you through the creation of all kinds of publications for desktop or commercial printing—even your own Web site! PagePlus ships with a selection of design templates, and many more are available on the PagePlus X3 Resource DVD.

Templates help ensure continuity between your publications by preserving starting setups for such elements as page layout, contents, styles, and colour palettes.

To create a publication from a design template:

1. Open PagePlus, or choose **New...** from the File menu and select **New from Startup Wizard...**.

2. Click **Use Design Template**.

3. In the **Templates** list on the left, select a publication category and then examine the samples on the right. Click the sample that is the closest match to the document you want to create and then click **Open**.

Starting a new publication from scratch

Although design templates can simplify your design choices, you can just as easily start out from scratch with a new, blank publication. To make life easier you can adopt a particular document type (regular/normal, folded, small/large publication, web page) as a starting point. Examples include greeting cards, banners, posters, and labels.

To start a new publication (via Startup Wizard):

1. Open PagePlus to display the initial Startup Wizard (if switched on).
   OR
   With PagePlus loaded, choose **New...** from the File menu and then select **New from Startup Wizard...**.

2. Select **Create>Start New Publication**.

3. In the **Templates** list on the left, select a document type and then examine the samples on the right. Click the sample that is the closest match to the document you want to create.
   OR
   You can define a custom publication by clicking **Custom Page Setup...**.

4. Click **Open** to open a new publication with a blank page.

> If you click ⊠ **Cancel** (or press **Escape**) from the Startup Wizard, PagePlus opens a blank document using default page properties.

To start a new default publication:

- Click the 🗋 **New Publication** button on the Standard toolbar (only if Startup Wizard is turned off).

Opening an existing publication

You can open an existing PagePlus publication from the Startup Wizard, Standard toolbar, or via the File menu.

It is also possible to Import PDF files via the Startup Wizard. Alternatively, the pages of an existing PagePlus publication can be inserted into a currently open publication before or after a currently selected page—use **Insert>PagePlus File...** from the Insert menu.

To open an existing publication from the Startup Wizard:

1. Select the **Open Saved Publication** option. In the Documents pane of the **Open Saved Work** dialog, you'll see either your computer's folder structure for navigation to your publications (Folders tab) or a list of most recently used PagePlus publications (History tab). Preview thumbnails or publication details can be shown in the adjacent pane depending on your current view.

2. Click a file name or sample, then click **Open**.

To open an existing publication from within PagePlus:

1. Click the 📂 **Open** button on the Standard toolbar.

2. In the Open dialog, select the folder and file name and click the **Open** button.

To revert to the saved version of an open publication:

- Choose **Revert** from the File menu.

Font substitution

PagePlus supports automatic font substitution as you open a PagePlus publication which has fonts which are not stored on your computer. The dialog that shows also lets you manually substitute a missing font if necessary. See PagePlus help for more details.

Importing PagePlus documents

It is possible to import any PagePlus document into your currently loaded PagePlus document, typically to reuse content. The character formatting, layout and images used in the original document are maintained to honour the look and feel of the original content. Pages are inserted into the currently open publication before or after a currently selected page, or can replace the current page.

To insert a PagePlus document into an existing PagePlus document:

1. Open your existing PagePlus document.
2. Select a page from the Pages tab (remember to double-click the page to select) or from the navigation buttons on the Hintline.
3. Choose **Insert>PagePlus File...** from the Insert menu.
4. In the Open dialog, navigate to and select the PagePlus document for insertion. Click **Open**.
5. From the **Insert PagePlus File** dialog, choose to insert the pages of the imported PagePlus document **Before the current page**, **On the current page**, or **After the current page**.
6. If necessary, check the options to group each new page as a single object and to resize your current publication to that of your inserted PagePlus document.
7. Click the **OK** button.

Importing PDF files

It is possible to import any PDF document created with other applications directly into PagePlus to create either a new PagePlus publication or to add to an existing publication. The character formatting, layout and images in the original PDF document are preserved to allow comprehensive editing of the document.

To honour the look and feel of an original PDF file, any font embedded in the original PDF (and which is used in imported text) is extracted from the imported PDF file and installed automatically. The document containing the imported

PDF content will only make the font available if it is embedded in the project. This is true of TrueType (TTF) fonts and OpenType fonts with TTF or Type 1 outlines, but PostScript Type 1 fonts themselves are not supported.

> The embedded font can't be used for other documents or applications and will not appear in the Windows Fonts folder.

The pages of a PDF document can be inserted into a currently open publication before or after a currently selected page, or can replace the current page.

To import a PDF file to create a PagePlus publication:

1. Click the 🗁 **Open** button on the Standard toolbar.

2. Select the name of the file, and click **Open**. The PDF document is imported and will repaginate to the number of pages of the original PDF document.

3. Click **OK**.

4. Use **File>Save** to save as a PagePlus publication (*.PPP).

To insert a PDF file into an existing PagePlus publication:

1. Open your existing PagePlus publication.

2. Select and view a page from the Pages tab by double-clicking (or from the navigation buttons on the Hintline).

3. Choose **Insert>PDF File...** from the Insert menu.

4. In the Open dialog, navigate to and select the PDF file for insertion. Click **Open**.

5. From the **Insert PDF File** dialog, choose to insert the pages of the imported PDF document **Before the current page**, **On the current page** or **After the current page**.

6. If necessary, check the options to group each new page as a single object and to resize your current publication to that of your inserted PDF document.

7. Click the **OK** button.

Working with more than one publication

PagePlus lets you open more than one publication at a time. Each new publication you open appears in a separate window with its own settings. With windows reduced or tiled you can also drag and drop objects between windows. You can also preview the current publication in a separate window (see *Previewing the printed page* on p. 204).

To close the current window:

- Choose **Close** from the File menu or click the window's ✕ **Close** button. If it's the only window open for the publication, the command closes the publication and you'll be prompted to save changes.

> You can close all open publications without exiting the main PagePlus application.

The Window menu lets you create new windows and arrange the open document windows in various ways, i.e. by cascading and tiling horizontally or vertically.

Saving your publication

To save your work:

- Click the 💾 **Save** button on the Standard toolbar.

- To save under a different name, choose **Save As...** from the File menu.

Closing the publication

To close the current window:

- Choose **Close** from the File menu or click the window's ✕ **Close** button. If it's the only window open for the publication, the command closes the publication and you'll be prompted to save changes.

To close PagePlus:

- Click the program's ✕ **Close** button at the top right of the window.
  OR
  Choose **Exit** from the File menu.

You'll be prompted to save changes to any open publications.

Updating and saving defaults

Object defaults are the stored property settings PagePlus applies to *newly created* text, graphics, and frames. When you create text in your publication, it will have default properties for font, size, colour, alignment, etc. New graphics will have default properties for line and fill colour, shade, pattern, etc. New frames will have default properties for margins, columns, etc. You can easily change the defaults for any type of object.

Default settings are always **local**—that is, any changed defaults apply to the current publication and are automatically saved with it, so they're in effect next time you open that publication. However, at any time you can use the Save Defaults command to record the current defaults as **global** settings that will be in effect for any new publication you subsequently create.

To set local defaults for a particular type of object:

1. Create a single sample object and fine-tune its properties as desired—or use an existing object that already has the right properties. (For graphics, you can use a line, shape, or rectangle; all share the same set of defaults.)

2. Select the object that's the basis for the new defaults and choose **Update Object Default** from the Format menu (or **Update Text Default** for text).

Or, for line and fill colours, including line styles:

3. With no object selected, choose the required line and/or fill colours from the Colour or Swatches tab. Use the Line tab to set a default line weight, style, and corner shape.

4. Draw your object on the page, which will automatically adopt the newly defined default colours and styles.

To view and change default text properties:

1. Choose **Text Style Palette...** from the Format menu.

2. Click **Default Text**, then click **Modify...** to view current settings.

3. Use the Text Style dialog to alter character, paragraph, or other properties.

To save all current defaults as global settings:

1. Choose **Save Defaults** from the Tools menu.

2. Click **OK** to confirm that you want new publications to use the current publication's defaults.

Working
with Pages

Setting up a publication

A publication's **page size** and **orientation** settings are fundamental to your layout, and are defined when the new publication is first created, either using a design template or as a New Publication choice via **File>New...** and the Startup Wizard. If the Startup Wizard is turned off, or you cancel the setup dialog, a new publication is created to a default page size.

To adjust size/orientation of the current publication:

1. On the **File** menu, choose **Page Setup...**.

2. For **Regular/Booklet** publications, you can select a pre-defined paper size or enter custom values for page width and height, as well as setting the orientation (Portrait or Landscape). For booklets only, select a type from the **Booklet** drop-down menu, which page to start on (left/right), and if you require **Facing pages** (including **Dual master pages**).

3. For other publication types, you can select the publication types: **Small** (for example, business cards, labels, etc.), **Large** (banners or posters), or **Folded** (booklets).

    *   For Small publications, either enable **Paper**, then create a custom paper size, or for creating **Labels**, enable the radio button and pick an Avery label code which matches your labels.

    *   For Large and Folded publications, choose a pre-defined option from the list (use the preview) or to define a custom publication based on the selected option, click the **Create Custom** button. Add additional custom settings if necessary.

4. Click **OK** to accept the new dimensions. The updated settings will be applied to the current publication.

Facing pages

You can set up your regular publication or booklet so that the PagePlus window displays pages either singly or in pairs—as two facing pages side by side. You'll need facing pages if you're creating a publication where you need to see both the left-hand (verso) and right-hand (recto) pages, or one that employs double-page spreads where a headline or other element needs to run from the left-hand page to the right-hand page.

If you set up a publication to use facing pages, you can specify either a **single** or **dual** master page. A single master page is (as the name implies) a single page; a dual master page is a spread with both a left- and right-page component, allowing you to run elements across the spread in the background of the publication, or position left-side page numbers and right-side page numbers at opposite corners. The Pages tab shows single master pages with a standard page thumbnail, and dual master pages with a split-page thumbnail.

To set up facing pages:

1. In the **Page Setup** dialog, check **Facing Pages**.

2. If you plan to use background elements that span a double-page spread, select **Dual master pages**. This will let you define master pages with paired "left page" and "right page" components.
   OR
   For a facing-page layout where both left and right pages initially share the same master page, and you don't need to run background elements across the spread, clear **Dual master pages**.

Because you assign master pages to individual page layers, one page at a time, it takes two separate steps to assign a dual master page to both left and right facing pages. For details, see Assigning master pages on p. 36.

You can assign different master pages to the left and right publication pages if necessary. For example (see below), a left-hand "body text" page might use the left-side component of one master page, while a right-hand "chapter divider" page could use the right side of a different master page.

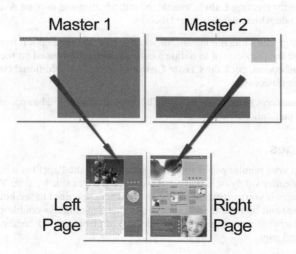

Master 1   Master 2

Left Page   Right Page

Understanding master pages

Master pages provide a flexible way to store background elements that you'd like to appear on more than one page—for example a logo, background, header/footer, or border design.

The key concept here is that a particular master page is typically **shared** by multiple pages, as illustrated below. By placing a design element on a master page and then assigning several pages to use that master page, you ensure that all the pages incorporate that element. Of course, each individual page can have its own "foreground" elements.

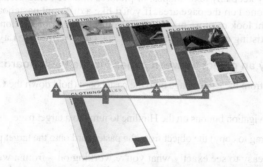

Master pages are available in every publication, but in a simple publication you may not need to use any master pages—or you may need only one master page. Facing pages and multiple master pages prove valuable with longer, more complex publications.

Using the **Pages** tab or **Page Manager**, you can quickly add or delete master pages; for example, you could set up different master pages for "title" or "chapter divider" pages. For details, see Adding, removing, and rearranging pages on p. 35.

Viewing pages

Most of the PagePlus display is taken up by a page or "artwork" area and a surrounding "pasteboard" area.

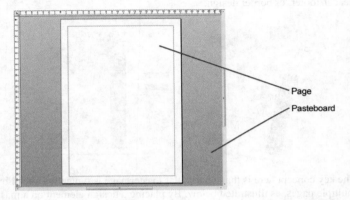

Page
Pasteboard

In PagePlus, the **page area** is where you put page layout guides, and of course the text, shapes, and pictures that you want to print. The **Pasteboard** area is where you generally keep any text, shapes, or pictures that are being prepared or waiting to be positioned on the page area. If you'd like a different pasteboard colour for a different look or more practically if your off-page objects don't contrast with the existing colour, you can set this via **Tools>Options>Layout**.

To move or copy an object between pages via the Pasteboard:

1. Drag the object from the source page onto the pasteboard (hold down the **Ctrl** key to copy).

2. Use the page navigation buttons on the Hintline to jump to a target page.

3. Drag (or **Ctrl**-drag to copy) the object from the pasteboard onto the target page.

PagePlus makes it easy to see exactly what you're working on—from a wide view of multiple pages to a close-up view of a small region. For example, you can use the **scroll bars** at the right and bottom of the main window to move the page and pasteboard with respect to the main window. If you're using a **wheel mouse**, you can scroll vertically by rotating the wheel, or horizontally by **Shift**-scrolling.

The View toolbar provides the:

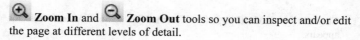 **Zoom In** and **Zoom Out** tools so you can inspect and/or edit the page at different levels of detail.

100% ▾ **Zoom Percent** option to set a level of magnification (expressed as a percentage).

Zoom Tool to zoom into an area defined by a drawn marquee selection.

Pan Tool for moving the page area by dragging.

Actual size option for viewing the page at its true size (100%).

Zoom to selection option to focus on a selected area.

Page Width option to fit to the page's width.

Full Page option to fit the page into your current window.

Multi-page option to view multiples pages simultaneously (set page number by dragging a page array from the flyout menu).

Switching view modes

You can switch between different view modes:

- **Normal** view, which displays one page at a time.

- **Multi-page** view, used for inspecting long documents, displays a number of pages according to a configurable page array (e.g., a 3x1 grid).

In Normal and Multi-page view, the pasteboard is shared by all pages. In Multi-page view, it's also especially easy to move or copy objects between pages using drag-and-drop and set the number of pages displayed.

> For any view, use the Pan Tool to quickly locate the area of interest in your publication.

To view multiple pages (in Multi-page mode):

1. Click the  **Multi-page** flyout on the View toolbar. An array selector appears.

2. Click and drag to choose an array within the selector, for example 2x4 Pages or 3x1 Pages (as shown). To expand the number of choices, drag down and to the right. Click **Normal View** if you change your mind.

The publication appears in Multi-page mode with the specified page array in view.

To switch between views:

- Choose between **Normal** or **Multi-page** from the View menu.

Navigating

To switch between pages:

- Click the ◀ **Previous Page**, ▶ **Next Page**, |◀ **First Page** or ▶| **Last Page** button on the Hintline.
  OR
  On the Studio's **Pages** tab, double-click the page's thumbnail for the page (or master page) you want to view. The lower Pages window of the tab displays normal pages, while the expandable Master Pages window shows only master pages.

> 💡 You may need to click the Master Pages ▶ button to display the master page thumbnails in their own window.

To switch between the master page and normal page:

- Click the Current Page box on the HintLine, e.g. 2 of 5 .
  OR
  Choose **Master Page** from the View menu (or **Page** to switch back).

To switch to a master page from a particular layer:

- From the Layers tab, right-click a particular layer's name and choose **Goto Master Page**.

Once you've displayed a page or master page, you can normally edit any object on it—regardless of which layer the object is on—simply by clicking the object. In order to create a new object on a particular layer, you'll first need to "activate" (switch to) that layer.

To switch to a particular layer of a page/master page:

- After displaying the page or master page, click at the very beginning of the chosen layer entry in the Layers tab.

The layer becomes active, and a ▶ mark appears next to its entry in the Layers tab.

Adding, removing, and rearranging pages

Use the **Pages tab** to quickly rearrange pages using drag-and-drop, and add or delete standard pages or master pages. The tab displays master pages in the upper (collapsible) **Master Pages** panel and standard publication pages in the lower **Pages** panel.

The ⊞ **Page Manager** button provides additional options, such as duplicating a particular page, assigning a specific master page, or adding/deleting multiple pages.

To add a single page:

1. On the **Pages** tab, click once to select a page in the **Pages** panel.

   Note: The thumbnail that's shown as "selected" is independent of the page you're currently working on. To work on a particular page, double-click its thumbnail.

2. Click the ⊞ **Add** button to add a page (or master page) *before* the one selected in the panel.
   OR
   To add a new page *at the end* of the publication, deselect all pages by clicking in the neutral grey region of the lower panel, then click the **Add** button.

To add master pages:

For master pages, the above procedure applies but within the Master Pages panel. The only exception is that you cannot create a new master page based on a design template's pages (no dialog opens).

To delete a single page/master page:

1. On the **Pages** tab, select the page (or master page) to delete on the appropriate panel by clicking its thumbnail.

2. Click the ⬛ **Remove** button.

To rearrange pages:

• On the **Pages** tab, in the lower **Pages** panel, drag a page thumbnail to a new location in the page sequence.

Assigning master pages to layers

Each layer you add to a regular page can use its own master page. If your publication uses more than one master page, you can reassign specific master pages to specific page layers at any time.

To assign a master page to a page layer:

1. On the **Layers** tab, double-click in the ⬚ **Master Page(s)** column of the chosen page layer.

2. In the **Select Master Page** dialog, select the normal page and master page from the drop-down menus.

Working with layers

Each new page or master page consists of a single **layer**. One layer may be enough to accommodate the elements of a particular layout, but you can create additional layers as needed. On each layer, objects such as text frames and pictures are stacked in the order you create them, from back to front, with each new object in front of the others. Layers themselves are stacked in a similar way, and of course you can juggle the order of objects and layers as needed.

Layers are useful when you're working on a complex design where it makes sense to separate one cluster of objects from another. You can work on one layer at a time without worrying about affecting elements on a different layer.

Once you've displayed a page, you can normally edit any object on it—regardless of which layer the object is on—simply by clicking the object.

Each layer is situated along with other layers (if present) within a stack on the Layers tab. The uppermost layer is applied over any lower layer on the page.

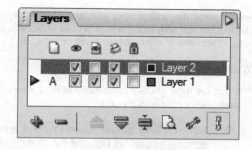

Layer 1 and Layer 2 above could represent the following:

To display the Layers tab:

- Go to **View>Studio Tabs** and select the **Layers** tab, if the tab is not visible.

In order to create new objects on a particular layer, you'll need to "activate" (switch to) that layer.

To activate a particular layer:

- From the **Layers** tab, click at the beginning of a layer entry to activate that layer. You'll see the ▶ layer arrow jump to the now activated layer (Layer 1 in the Layers tab example above is currently active).

Don't confuse this with simply selecting a layer (Layer 2 in the example is selected, but not activated), which is used to manage the layer itself (e.g., to move it, preview it, view/change layer options, etc.).

To select a particular layer:

- Click (or right-click) a layer name in the **Layers** tab. The layer entry then possesses a blue background.

> ● Right-clicking a layer name displays a menu of layer-related actions, as well as Options for that particular layer.

Adding, removing, and rearranging layers

When you add a new page or master page to the publication, you can specify whether to copy the layers and/or objects from a particular source page. Once you've created a page, it's easy to add, delete, move, or merge layers as needed. Moving a layer will place its objects in front or in back of those on other layers.

To add a new layer to the current page or master page:

1. In the Layers tab, click the **Insert new layer** button.
2. You'll be prompted to give the new layer a name and set its properties. When you've made your selections, click **OK**.

To delete a layer:

- In the Layers tab, select the layer's name and click the **Delete selected layer(s)** button.

You can move layers up or down in the stacking order to place their objects in front or behind those on other layers, move objects to specific layers, and even merge layers.

To move a layer in the stacking order:

- In the Layers tab, select the layer's entry, then click the **Move layer up** or **Move layer down** button to move the layer up or down in the list, respectively.

To move an object to a specific layer:

- Select the object and choose **Send to Layer** from the Arrange menu, then select the destination layer from the submenu.

To merge one layer with another in the Layers tab:

1. Activate the layer you want to merge to by clicking its entry. A ► mark indicates that the layer is active. (Note that the active layer becomes uppermost in the workspace.)

2. ▼ Select the entry of the layer you want to merge, and click the **Merge into active layer** button.

The contents of the merged layer appear on the active layer.

Selecting objects on layers

Once you've displayed a page or master page, you can normally select and then edit any object on it—regardless of which layer the object is on—simply by clicking the object. Alternatively, you can limit object selection and editing to objects on a specific active layer.

To edit only objects on the active layer:

- ▫ In the Layers tab, select the chosen layer (the ► mark should show next to the active layer) and uncheck **Edit all layers**.

To select all objects on a particular layer:

- In the Layers tab, right-click the chosen layer and choose **Select All Objects**.

Normally the active layer stays the same regardless of which object you select. For ease in identifying which layer a given object resides on, the object's **selection handles** will be coloured according to the layer it resides on; the layer colour is shown in the Layers tab (see Layer names and properties on p. 41) and is configurable.

Layers and master pages

Master pages are special "background" pages that can be shared by more than one regular page. They are assigned to **each layer** of a regular page rather than to the page as a whole—so if a page has multiple layers it can also employ multiple master pages! For example, one master page might include background text elements, while another included background graphics. By assigning the two master pages to separate layers you could achieve a unified design while keeping the elements separate. Page layers can each take a master page, but master page layers cannot.

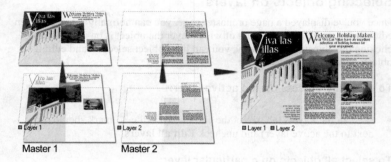

Master 1   Master 2

You can also set any layer to use no master page. Commonly, the first layer uses a master page while subsequent layers use no master page, but there's no hard and fast rule. You can assign the master page either when you first create the layer, or subsequently, as the layout evolves.

To assign a master page to a page layer:

1. In the Layers tab, double-click in the ⬜ **Master Page(s)** column of the chosen page layer.

2. In the **Select Master Page** dialog, select the normal page and master page from the displayed drop-down menus. The master page letter (e.g., A, B, C, etc.) is shown on the chosen layer when assigned.

Master pages, like regular pages, can have more than one layer. Layers on master pages work almost exactly like those on regular pages. The key difference is that master page layers cannot themselves take a master page; master pages can only be assigned to layers on regular pages.

When you add a new master page to the publication, you have the option of copying the layers and/or objects from an existing master page. If you choose not to copy existing layers, the new master page starts out with one layer. You can always add more as described above.

Layer names and properties

The Layers tab and associated Layer Options dialog let you set a variety of properties for one or more layers. It is possible to rename the layer, make the layer and objects on it visible/invisible, set the layer to not to print, lock layers (to prevent accidental changes to objects), or set a selection handle colour (to help identify which objects belong to which layer).

To set layer properties:

1. Display the Layers tab.

2. Select desired settings for the chosen layer.

   - Check the box in the ⬜ **Master Page(s)** column to assign a normal and/or master page to the layer.

   - Check the box in the ✱ **Visible** column to show the layer and any objects on it; uncheck to hide the layer.

   - Check the box in the 🖾 **Master Page(s) visible** column to show the layer's master page; uncheck to hide it.

   - Check the ✎ **Printable** column to include the layer in page printouts; uncheck to exclude it.

   - Check the box in the 🔒 **Locked** column to prevent objects on the layer from being selected/edited; uncheck to allow editing.

- To set the **Selection handle colour**, click the colour selection button and choose a colour from the palette (click **More Colours...** for a wider choice).

If required, you can click the **Layer Options** button instead.

To toggle all layer properties:

- Choose **All Layers Visible**, **All Layers Printable**, or **All Layers Locked** from the View menu.

> You can also toggle **View/Master Page Objects** to show/hide master page objects.

Setting guides for page margins, rows, columns, and bleeds

Layout guides are visual guide lines that help you position layout elements. They can include **page margins**, **row and column guides**, **bleed area guides**, and **ruler guides**.

Page margin settings are fundamental to your layout, and usually are among the first choices you'll make after starting a publication from scratch. The page margins are shown as a blue box which is actually four guide lines—for top, bottom, left, and right—indicating the underlying page margin settings. If you like, you can set the margins to match your current printer settings.

You also have the option of setting up **row** and **column guides** as an underlying layout aid. PagePlus represents rows and columns on the page area with dashed blue guide lines. Unlike the dashed grey frame margins and columns, row and column guides don't control where frame text flows. Rather, they serve as visual aids that help you match the frame layout to the desired column layout.

Bleed area guides assist you in positioning "bleed" elements that you want to run to the edge of a trimmed page. To allow for inaccuracies in the trimming process in professional printing, it's a good idea to extend these elements beyond the "trim edge"—the dimensions defined by your Page Setup.

With bleed guides switched on, the page border expands by a distance you specify, and the trim edge is shown with dashed lines and little "scissors" symbols. Note that these guide lines are just a visual aid; only the Bleed limit setting in the Print dialog extends the actual output page size.

You can also define free-floating red ruler guides by clicking and dragging from the PagePlus rulers. See Creating ruler guides on p. 46.

Defining layout guides

To define layout guides:

- Click ⊞ Layout Guides on the Page context toolbar, **Layout Guides...** from the File menu, or right-click on a blank part of the page and choose **Layout Guides**. Then in the **Layout Guides** dialog, use the **Margins** tab to set guide lines for page margins, rows and columns, and bleed areas.

  - In the **Margin Guides** section, you can set the left, right, top, and bottom page margins individually, or click the **From Printer** button to derive the page margin settings from the current printer settings. The dialog also provides options for **Balanced margins** (left matching right, top matching bottom) or for **Mirrored margins** on facing pages where the "left" margin setting becomes the "inside," and the "right" margin becomes the "outside."

  - Use the **Row and Column Guides** section to define guides for rows and columns. If you want rows or columns of uneven width, first place them at fixed intervals, then drag to reposition them as required.

  - Use **Bleed area guides** to specify the extra margin you want to allow around the original Page Setup dimensions or "trim area." Note that if the setting is zero or you have **View>Bleed Area Guides** unchecked, you won't see the bleed area displayed.

To show or hide layout guides:

- On the **View** menu, check or uncheck **Guide Lines**.

To show or hide bleed area guides:

- On the **View** menu, check or uncheck **Bleed Area Guides**.

Sticky guides

Guides are normally "sticky" in that objects snapped to them will be moved when the guide is moved across/down the page. Objects stuck to guides can be unstuck individually at any time or the whole feature can be switched off.

To make individual objects "non-sticky":

1. Select the object.
2. Click one of two small red triangular markers shown at the point where the object is attached to the guide. You'll see a link cursor (🔗) as you hover over the sticky guide marker.

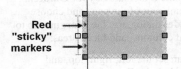

Red "sticky" markers

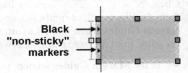

Black "non-sticky" markers

Click red marker to make non-sticky.

Markers become non-sticky and change to black.

If you then drag the red guide away the object will not follow.

> You can make the object stick to a guide again by offering it up to the guide line.

To turn sticky guides on and off:

*   Check/uncheck **Sticky Guides** from the Arrange menu (or the equivalent from **Tools>Options>Layout**).

Previously stuck objects will remain sticky even after sticky guides are switched off—you'll have to make them non-sticky manually.

Using the rulers and dot grid

The PagePlus **rulers** mimic the paste-up artist's T-square, and serve several purposes:

*   To act as a measuring tool.
*   To create ruler guides for aligning and snapping.
*   To set and display tab stops (see p. 95).
*   To set and display paragraph indents (see p. 94).

Ruler units

To select the basic measurement unit used by the rulers:

- Choose **Options...** from the Tools menu and select the **Rulers** page.

In Paper Publishing mode, the default unit is inches or centimetres; in Web Publishing mode, the default is pixels.

Adjusting rulers

By default, the horizontal ruler lies along the top of the PagePlus window and the vertical ruler along the left edge. The default **ruler intersection** is the top-left corner of the pasteboard area. The default **zero point** (marked as 0 on each ruler) is the top-left corner of the page area. (Even if you have set up bleed area guides and the screen shows an oversize page, the zero point stays in the same place, i.e. the top-left corner of the trimmed page.)

Ruler Intersection

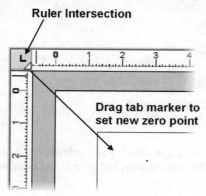

Drag tab marker to set new zero point

To define a new zero point:

- Drag the tab marker on the ruler intersection to a new zero point on the page or pasteboard. (Be sure to click only the triangular marker!)

To move the rulers:

- With the **Shift** key down, drag the tab marker on the ruler intersection. The zero point remains unchanged.

- Double-click on the ruler intersection to make the rulers and zero point jump to the top left-hand corner of the currently selected object. This comes in handy for measuring page objects.

To restore the original ruler position and zero point:

- Double-click the tab marker on the ruler intersection.

To lock the rulers and prevent them from being moved:

- Choose **Tools>Options...** and select the **Rulers** page, then check **Lock Rulers**.

Rulers as a measuring tool

The most obvious role for rulers is as a measuring tool. As you move the mouse pointer, small lines along each ruler display the current horizontal and vertical cursor position. When you click to select an object, shaded ruler regions indicate the object's left/right and top/bottom edges on the horizontal and vertical rulers, respectively. Each region has a zero point relative to the object's upper left corner, so you can see the object's dimensions at a glance.

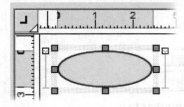

Creating ruler guides

PagePlus lets you to set up horizontal and vertical **ruler guides**—non-printing, red lines you can use to align headlines, pictures, and other layout elements.

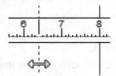

Guides are by default "sticky" so that stuck objects can be dragged around the page by their ruler guide—a great way to move previously aligned objects in bulk and simultaneously. You can choose to make objects stick to a guide or unstick them, or even switch sticky guides off completely. (See Sticky guides on p. 44).

- To create a ruler guide, click on a ruler, hold down your mouse button, then drag onto your page. A red ruler guide line appears parallel to the ruler (**Alt**-drag to create the guide at 90 degrees to the ruler).

- To move a guide, drag it.

- To remove a guide, drag and drop it anywhere outside the page area.

- To lock ruler guides, on the **Tools** menu, click **Options...** and select the **Layout** menu option, then check **Lock guide lines**.

- To fine-position ruler guides, choose **Layout Guides...** from the File menu (or right-click menu) and select the **Guides** tab. Here, you can create or delete individual guides.

- To switch off sticky guides, uncheck **Sticky Guides** on the Arrange menu.

- To send guides to the back (for clearer object editing), on the **Tools** menu, click **Options...**, select the **Layout** menu option, then check the **Guide lines to back** option.

- By default, guides are red but you can swap to any other colour via **Tools>Options>Layout**—simply pick a new Guide Colour. By checking **Use Layer Colour** from the same location your guides can instead adopt the currently selected layer's colour. Switching off the layer in the Layers tab will hide the guides for that layer.

Using the dot grid

The **dot grid** is a matrix of dots or lines based on ruler units, covering the page and pasteboard areas. Like ruler guides, it's handy for both visual alignment and snapping.

- To turn the dot grid on or off, click **Dot Grid** on the View menu.
  OR
  Choose **Options...** from the Tools menu and select the **Snapping** menu option. Check or uncheck **Dot Grid**.

You can also set the grid spacing, style, colour, and positioning in the dialog (see PagePlus help).

Using headers and footers

Headers and footers are layout elements that are positioned at the top and bottom of your master page(s), and are repeated on every page of your publication. The **Headers and Footers Wizard** lets you create these elements easily.

To create headers and/or footers:

- On the Insert menu, choose **Headers and Footers...** and follow the Wizard instructions. The header and/or footer is automatically applied to the master page (and not the current page).

To edit existing headers and footers:

- On the Insert menu, choose **Headers and Footers....** In the **Headers and Footers Wizard**, select **Edit header**, **Leave header as it is**, or **Delete header** and then complete the Wizard instructions. Carry out the equivalent operation for your footer if needed.

Using page numbering

Page number fields automatically display the current page number. Typically, these fields are added automatically to the master page (so they appear on every page) with the Header and Footers Wizard, but you can insert a page number field anywhere in your text.

You can change the style of page numbers, the page on which numbering begins, and number continuation across chapters (all via **Page Number Format** on the Format menu).

To define a header or footer that includes a page number field:

1. Create a header or footer on the master page by choosing **Headers and Footers...** from the Insert menu.

2. In the wizard, press the **Page Number** button to insert a page number field (as a prefix or suffix) along with any optional header/footer text.

3. Complete the wizard.

To insert a page number field:

1. Switch to the master page (if desired) by clicking the Current Page box on the Hintline.

2. Create a new text object. Inside the text object, click for an insertion point to place the page number.

3. On the Insert menu, choose **Page Number**.

To change page numbering style:

1. On the Format menu, choose **Page Number Format...**.

2. In the **Page Number Format** dialog, in the **Style** section, you can select from various standard numbering schemes such as Arabic numerals (1, 2, 3...) or Upper Roman (I, II, III...).

   You can also specify the **First Page Number** in the sequence (this will appear on the first page of the publication). For example, Chapter Two of a long publication might be in a separate file and begin numbering with page 33.

Working
with Objects

Selecting an object

Before you can change any object, you need to select it using one of these tools from the Tools toolbar:

Pointer Tool
Click to use the **Pointer Tool** to select, move, copy, resize or rotate objects.

Rotate Tool
Click to use the **Rotate Tool** to rotate an object around a rotation origin (normally centred). Select the object, then drag one of its handles. You can also use the Rotate Tool to move and copy objects. See Rotating an object on p. 64.

To select an object:

- Click on the object using one of the tools shown above. A grey bounding box appears, with small "handles" defining the object's corners and edges.

  The object also shows an attached **Move** button which lets you drag the selected object to a new position.

- If objects overlap, **Alt**-click until the desired object is selected.

When selecting a text object with the Pointer Tool:

- Clicking on a text object with the Pointer Tool selects the object and also positions the blinking text selection cursor within the object's text. In this mode, you can edit the text.

- Double-click to select a word, and triple-click to select a paragraph.

- Press the **Delete** key to delete characters after the cursor. To delete the frame itself, choose **Delete Object** from the Edit menu (or **Ctrl**-Delete).

To select only the frame (for example, to adjust its margin and column guides), click the frame's bounding box.

Simply clicking on any member of a group selects the group object. In general, any operation you carry out on a selected group affects each member of the group. However, you can also select and edit an individual object within a group.

To select an individual object within a group:

- **Ctrl**-click the object.

Selecting multiple objects

Selecting more than one object at a time (creating a **multiple selection**) lets you:

- Position or resize all the objects at the same time.

- Create a **group object** from the multiple selection, which can then be treated as a single object, with the option of restoring the individual objects later. See Creating groups on p. 56.

To create a multiple selection:

- Click in a blank area of the page and drag a "marquee" box around the objects you want to select. Repeated **Shift**-drags add to the selection region.
  OR
  Hold down the **Shift** key and click each object in turn.

To add or remove an object from a multiple selection:

- Hold down the **Shift** key and click the object to be added or removed.

To deselect all objects in a multiple selection:

- Click in a blank area of the page.

To select all objects on the page (or master page):

- Choose **Select>Select All** from the Edit menu (or press **Ctrl+A**).

To select all objects of one type on the page (or master page):

- Hold down the **Ctrl** key and double-click one object of that type.
  OR
  Select one object then choose **Select>Select Similar** on the Edit menu.

To select all objects on a layer:

- Display the Layers tab, choose the layer name and right-click to **Select All Objects**.

Snapping

The **snapping** feature simplifies placement and alignment by "magnetizing" grid dots and guide lines. When snapping is on, the edges and centres of objects you create, move, or resize will jump to align with the nearest visible grid dot or guides. Objects normally snap to the page edge too.

Guide lines include ruler guides as well as layout guide lines based on page margins, rows, columns, and bleeds (see Setting guides for page margins, rows, columns, and bleeds on p. 42).

You may notice that with snapping enabled, when you move a guide, any "snapped to" objects will move with the guide. This object "stickiness" is enabled by default (with the Sticky Guides feature) but can be disabled permanently or temporarily as necessary (in **Tools>Options>Layout**). It is especially useful for selectively repositioning objects in bulk by guide movement, without any unnecessary grouping operations.

To turn snapping on and off:

- Click the ⊞ **Snapping** button on the Hintline. When the button is down, snapping is on.

Selective snapping

You control which points and lines are snapped to by showing or hiding the individual guide elements (i.e., Rulers, Guide Lines, Frames, Dot Grid, etc.), and by changing options settings for those visible elements.

To show or hide guide elements:

- Enable (or disable) the element from the View menu.
  OR
  Check (or uncheck) the element's name from **Tools>Options>Layout**.
  OR
  Right-click on the page or pasteboard and choose **View**, then select the element's name.

To set which visible elements are snapped to:

1. Choose **Options...** from the Tools menu.

2. Under "Snap to:" on the Snapping option, uncheck any elements you don't want to snap to. The choices include **Grid dots**, **Page/Bleed edge**, **Page margins**, **Ruler guides**, **Row/column guides**, **Nearest Pixel**, and **Ruler Marks**.

Creating groups

You can easily turn a multiple selection into a group object. When objects are grouped, you can position, resize, or rotate the objects all at the same time.

To create a group from a multiple selection:

- Click the **Group** button below the selection.

To ungroup:

- Click the **Ungroup** button below the selection to turn back to a multiple selection.

Simply clicking on any member of a group selects the group object. In general, any operation you carry out on a selected group affects each member of the group. However, the objects that comprise a group are intact, and you can also select and edit an individual object within a group.

To select an individual object within a group:

- **Ctrl**-click the object.

Copying, pasting, and replicating objects

Besides using the Windows Clipboard to copy and paste objects, you can duplicate objects easily using drag-and-drop, and replicate multiple copies of any object in precise formations. You can also transfer the formatting of one object to another, with the option of selecting specific attributes to be included when formatting is pasted.

To copy an object (or multiple selection) to the Windows Clipboard:

- Click the **Copy** button on the Standard toolbar.

If you're using another Windows application, you can usually copy and paste objects via the Clipboard.

To paste an object from the Clipboard:

- Click the **Paste** button on the Standard toolbar.

The standard Paste command inserts the object at the insertion point or (for a separate object) at the centre of the page. To insert a separate object at the same page location as the copied item, use the **Paste in Place** command.

To choose between alternative Clipboard formats:

- Choose **Paste Special...** from the Edit menu.

To duplicate an object:

1. Select the object, then press the **Ctrl** key.

2. Drag the outline to a new location on the page. You can release the **Ctrl** key to place the duplicated object.

3. To constrain the position of the copy (to same horizontal or vertical), press and hold down the **Shift** key while dragging. A duplicate of the object appears at the new location.

Replicating objects

Duplicating an object means making just one copy at a time. The **Replicate** command lets you create multiple copies in a single step, with precise control over how the copies are arranged, either as a linear series or a grid. You can include one or more transformations to produce an interesting array of rotated and/or resized objects. It's great for repeating backgrounds, or for perfectly-aligned montages of an image or object.

To replicate an object:

1.   Select the object to be replicated and choose **Replicate...** from the Edit menu. The Replicate dialog appears, with a preview region at the right.

2.   To arrange copies in a straight line, select **Create line**. For an X-by-Y grid arrangement, select **Create grid**.

3.   **Specify Line length** (the number of objects including the original) in the arrangement, or the Grid size. Note that you can use the Line length setting to include an odd number of objects in a grid.

4.   Set spacing between the objects as either an **Offset** (measured between the top left corners of successive objects) or a **Gap** (between the bottom right and top left corners). You can specify **Horizontal** and/or **Vertical** spacing, and/or an angular **Rotation**. To set a specific horizontal or vertical interval, check **Absolute**; uncheck the box to specify the interval as a percentage of the original object's dimensions.

5.   Click **OK**.

The result is a multiple selection. Click its ⌗ **Group** button if you want to keep the separate objects linked for additional manipulations.

Pasting an object's formatting

Once you have copied an object to the Clipboard, you can use **Paste Format** to apply its formatting attributes to another object. Another command, **Paste Format Plus**, displays a "master control" dialog that lets you optionally select or deselect specific attributes to be included when formatting is pasted. See the PagePlus Help for more information on the Paste Format Plus feature.

To paste one object's formatting to another:

1.   Copy the source object.

2.   Select the target object and choose **Paste Format** from the Edit menu.

The target object takes on any formatting attributes and settings of the source object.

Moving objects

To move an object (including a multiple selection):

- ⊕ Drag the selected object to a new position by using its **Move** button.
  OR
  Click within the object (not on a handle) and drag it to the new location
  while holding down the left mouse button.
  OR
  Drag the object's grey bounding box.

To constrain the movement of an object to horizontal or vertical:

- Select the object and use the keyboard arrows (up, down, left, right).
  OR
  Press and hold down the **Shift** key after you begin dragging the object.

  If you're looking for absolute positioning, you can move objects precisely with
  the Transform tab (See PagePlus Help).

Resizing objects

PagePlus provides several methods of resizing objects. Click-and-drag is the
simplest—watch the Hintline for context-sensitive tips and shortcuts! For
extremely precise resizing, use the Transform tab.

To resize an object (in general):

1. Select the object.

2. Click one of the selection handles and drag it to a new position while holding
   down the left mouse button.

Dragging from an edge handle resizes in one dimension, by moving that edge.
Dragging from a corner handle resizes in two dimensions, by moving two edges,
while maintaining the selection's aspect ratio (if needed).

Use centre snapping to scale an object in two directions simultaneously. Centre
snapping involves snapping to the object edge, then dragging from a corner (or
edge) handle.

> Text in frames and tables doesn't change size when the
> container object is resized.

> To set two or more objects to the same horizontal or vertical
> size as the last selected object, you can use **Arrange>Size
> Objects...**.

To resize freely:

- Drag from a corner (or line end) handle.

To constrain a shape, frame object, or table object when resizing:

- Hold the **Shift** key down and drag from a corner (or line end) handle.

Resizing groups and multiple selections

You can resize grouped objects or multiply selected objects. The size of images, graphic objects, and text objects in the group/selection will change.

If you're looking for absolute control, you can resize objects precisely with the Transform tab (See PagePlus help).

Locking an object's size or position

To prevent accidentally moving, resizing, flipping, or rotating an object, you can lock it in position.

To lock an object:

- Right-click on the object and choose **Arrange>Lock Objects**, or select the command from the Arrange menu.

To unlock an object:

- Right-click on it and choose **Arrange>Unlock Objects**, or choose the command from the Arrange menu.

Ordering objects

Each new page or master page consists of a single layer. One layer may be enough to accommodate the elements of a particular layout, but you can create additional layers as needed. On each layer, objects such as text frames and pictures are **stacked** in the order you create them, from back to front, with each new object in front of the others. You can change the stacking order, which affects how objects appear on the page.

To change the object's position in the stacking order:

- Select the object.

Then:

- ⬛ To shift the selected object's position to the bottom of the stack, use the **Send to Back** button on the Arrange toolbar.

- ⬛ To shift the selected object's position to the top of the stack, use the **Bring to Front** button on the Arrange toolbar.

- To shift the object's position one step toward the front, right-click on the object and choose **Arrange>Forward One**.

- To shift the object's position one step toward the back, right-click on the object and choose **Arrange>Back One**.

Aligning and distributing objects

Alignment involves taking a group of selected objects and aligning them all in one operation—the operation is applied to all of the objects selected. You can perform the following:

- Align edges of any two or more objects with one another. For example, top alignment will align objects to the top edge of the top-most object in the selection. Bottom alignment would align to the bottom edge of the bottom-most object.

- Space objects out at certain intervals. Lets you distribute objects, so that your objects (as a multiple selection) are spread evenly between the endmost objects on your page. Alternatively, check the **Spaced** option and corresponding measurement value to set a specific distance between each object.

- Align objects with the page margin or edge. Rather than work within the current selection area you can align to page margins (if set) or just the page edge.

It's also possible to align a single object either to the top, bottom, left, or right page edge or centre the object vertically or horizontally.

Alignment controls are available in either the Align tab or from **Arrange>Align Objects...**.

As another alignment option, layout tools such as **rulers**, **guide lines**, and **dot grid** provide guides to assist you in placing objects on the page. Snapping lets you align objects against sticky or non-sticky guides. For details, see Setting guides for page margins, rows, columns, and bleeds.

To align the edges of two or more objects:

1. Using the Pointer Tool, **Shift**-click on all the objects you want to align, or draw a marquee box around them, to create a multiple selection.

2. Select the Align tab.

3. Select an option for vertical and/or horizontal alignment. Choose **Top**, **Bottom**, **Left**, **Right**, **Centre Horizontally** or **Centre Vertically**, i.e.

To distribute two or more objects:

- Choose   **Space Evenly Across** or   **Space Evenly Down** to spread selected objects uniformly across the either the whole page (horizontally or vertically, respectively) or by a set measurement (choose **Spaced** and set a value in any measurement unit).

To align one or more objects with the page margins:

- Follow the steps above, but check **Include margins**. (If only one object is selected, the option is checked by default.)

Exporting as a picture

Exporting as a picture lets you convert all the objects on the page, or just the currently selected object(s), to an image file, using a file format you specify. It's particularly useful for generating logos and pictures to be used in publications created in other applications, such as a word processor.

PagePlus lets you export all or selected objects in **Serif Metafile Format** (.SMF). This proprietary format, an improvement on the Windows Metafile Format (WMF) due to improved text, line and fill handling, is especially useful for interworking between Serif products, i.e. you may want to utilize PagePlus objects in another Serif application to save time. The object is converted to a graphic and becomes non-editable, but the object's original appearance will be honoured. PagePlus can import Serif metafiles exported from other Serif applications as well as export them. (See Importing pictures on p. 147).

To export as a picture:

1. (If exporting objects, not the whole page) Select the object or **Shift**-click (or drag a marquee) to select multiple objects.

2. Choose **Export As Picture...** from the File menu.

3. In the **Save as type** drop-down list, select a image format, e.g. **Serif MetaFile Format (*.smf)**.

4. Specify a folder and file name for the picture.

5. To export just selected object(s), check **Selected object(s)**. To export the whole page, uncheck this box.

6. To choose from export options such as resolution, colour, and transparency, check **Show Filter Options**.

7. Click **Save**. You'll see export options, if available and requested, for the particular export filter in use.

Exporting Serif Metafiles

PagePlus lets you export pictures in Serif Metafile Format (.SMF). This proprietary format, an improvement on the Windows Metafile Format (WMF) due to improved text, line and fill handling, is especially useful for interworking between Serif products, i.e. you may want to utilize PagePlus objects in another Serif application to save time and effort. The object is converted to a graphic and becomes non-editable, but the object's original appearance will be honoured.

Rotating an object

You can rotate single and multiple objects, including pictures, text objects, and groups using the Rotate Tool.

To rotate an object:

1. Select the 🔄 **Rotate Tool** on the Tools toolbar's Selection flyout.

2. Click to select the object, hover over one of its handles until you see the rotate cursor (below).

3. Hold the mouse button down and drag the cursor in the direction in which you want to rotate the object, then release (use the **Shift** key for 15° rotation intervals).

The Pointer Tool can also be used to rotate objects in the same way (with the ↱ cursor).

To undo rotation (restore the original orientation):

- Double-click the object.

- To restore the rotated position, double-click again.

To change the rotation origin:

1. Select the 🔄 **Rotate Tool** and click to select the object.

2. Move the rotation origin ⊕ away from its original position in the centre of an object to any position on the page. The origin can also be moved to be outside the object—ideal for rotating grouped objects around a central point.

3. Drag the rotate pointer to a new rotation angle—the object will rotate about the new pivot.

To rotate an object 90 degrees left or right:

- Select the object and click the ◁ **Rotate Left** or ▷ **Rotate Right** button on the Arrange toolbar.

Flipping an object

You can flip objects horizontally (left to right; top and bottom stay the same) or vertically (top to bottom; left and right stay the same).

To flip an object horizontally/vertically:

- Select the object and choose **Flip Horizontal** or **Flip Vertical** from the Arrange menu.

Cropping and combining objects

Cropping means masking (hiding) parts of an object, for example to improve composition or create a special effect. The underlying object remains intact.

Several cropping techniques are available to the user:

- You can use either the **Square** or **Irregular Crop Tool** to adjust the object's crop outline.

- Use the **Crop to Shape** command, which lets you crop one object to the outline of another.

- The **Combine Curves** command, like Crop to Shape, starts with more than one object, but creates a special composite object with one or more "holes" on the inside where the component objects' fills overlapped one another— useful for creating mask or stencil effects.

- You can **rotate** a cropped object.

- You can apply feathering to the crop outline for a subtle edge softening, especially useful when overlapping objects (e.g. for vignetting effects).

To crop using the object's original outline:

1. Select the object, then select the ⊡ **Square Crop Tool** on the Attributes toolbar's Crop flyout.

2. Drag one of the object's edge or corner handles inward.

To crop by modifying the object's outline:

- Select the object and select the ⊠ **Irregular Crop Tool** on the Attributes toolbar's Crop flyout. The Curve context toolbar appears, and you'll see the nodes and connecting segments that define the object's crop outline.

- To move a node (control point) where you see the ⁻ᵢ⁻ cursor, drag the node.

- ↖⤿ To move a line segment (between two nodes) where you see the cursor, drag the segment.

- ✪ To convert an outline from straight lines to curves, click the **Fit Curves** button on the Curve context toolbar.

- To adjust the curvature of a segment, drag the control handle(s) of the adjacent nodes.

- ╬ ╼ To add or delete nodes for more or less complex outlines, select a node and click the **Add Node** or **Delete Node** button on the Curve context toolbar.

To position a cropped object within its crop outline:

- With either crop tool selected, click the object and drag its centre (when you see the hand cursor).

To resize objects within the crop outline:

- Select the object and with the **Square Crop Tool** enabled, **Ctrl**-drag either upwards or downwards to increase or decrease object size, respectively.

To feather the crop outline:

- With either crop tool selected, click the object.

- From the Crop context toolbar, set a **Feather** value using the up/down arrows, slider or by direct input. Feathering is applied outside the crop outline by the set point size.

To uncrop (restore full visibility):

- Click the ▱ **Remove Crop** button on the Attributes toolbar's Crop flyout.

Cropping one shape to another

The **Crop to Shape** command works with exactly two objects selected. Either or both of these may be a group object. The lower object (the one behind the other) gets clipped to the outline of the upper object, leaving a shape equivalent to the overlapping region. Note that you can't crop a mesh-warped object, but can use one to crop another object. Use **Combine Curves** to use one shape to punch a "hole" in another.

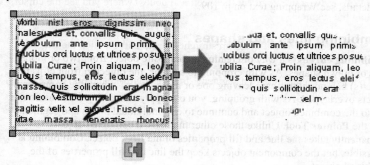

To crop one shape to another:

1. Place the "clipping" object in front of the object to be cropped, using the Arrange menu and/or Arrange toolbar as needed. In the illustration above, a QuickShape is in front of a text frame.

2. Choose **Crop to Shape** from the Tools menu to cut out the obscured underlying text.

You can restore an object cropped in this way to its original shape, but the upper "cropping" object is permanently deleted (use **Undo** to recover it if necessary).

Cropping to the wrap outline

Objects other than inline pictures have a **wrap outline** which determines how text flow changes if the object overlaps a text frame. Initially the wrap outline is set to match the crop outline, but for adjustment purposes the two are independent unless you specify that the crop outline should match the wrap outline. If you're planning to wrap text around an object and also need to crop it somewhat, it will save effort to adjust the wrap outline first, then set the crop outline to match.

To crop a selected object to its wrap outline:

1. Click the 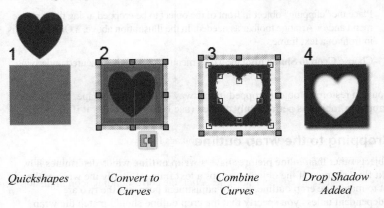 **Wrap Settings...** button on the Arrange toolbar, or choose **Wrap Settings...** from the Arrange menu.
   OR
   Right-click the object and choose **Wrap Settings...**.

2. Check the **Crop object to wrap outline** box.

For details, see Wrapping text on p. 109.

Combining lines and shapes

Combining curves is a way of creating a composite object from two or more lines or drawn shapes. As with cropping to a shape, the object in front clips the object(s) behind, in this case leaving one or more "holes" where the component objects overlapped. As with grouping, you can apply formatting (such as line or fill) to the combined object and continue to edit individual nodes and segments with the **Pointer Tool**. Unlike those other methods, a combined object permanently takes the line and fill properties of the front object. Combining is reversible, but the component objects keep the line and fill properties of the combined object.

Combining is a quick way to create a mask or stencil cutout:

Quickshapes	*Convert to Curves*	*Combine Curves*	*Drop Shadow Added*

To combine two or more selected lines or drawn shapes:

1. Draw your two lines or QuickShapes.

2. Place the "clipping" object in front of the object to be cut out, using the Arrange menu and/or Arrange toolbar as needed.

3. Select each object and choose **Tools>Convert To>Curves** for both.

4. Select both objects.

5. Choose **Combine Curves** from the Arrange menu.

> Combining doesn't work with QuickShapes or text objects. Use **Tools>Convert To>Curves** if necessary to first convert these objects to nodes and segments.

To restore the original shapes from a combined object:

- Select it and choose **Split Curves** from the Arrange menu.

Adding borders

A **border** is a repeating, decorative element that can be set to enclose an object. Borders work especially well with imported pictures.

To add a border to an object:

1. Click **Line/Border** on the Tools toolbar's Fill flyout.

2. To apply the border to specific edges of the object, use the **Border Edges** tab.

   - To select all edges or no edges, click the corresponding icon in the top row.

   - To toggle a single edge, click the corresponding icon in the bottom row.

     The preview at the left indicates with bolding which edges of the selected object will be updated with the current **Border** tab settings when you click **OK**.

3. To define the border, select the **Border** tab. In the **Side** list, select a border preset. You can preview each border in the window at the right. To remove a border, select **None**.

4. To match the corner pattern to the sides, leave **Keep side and corners the same** checked. To mix and match, uncheck the box and select a preset from the **Corner** list.

5. Choose an **Alignment** setting to fit the border to the **Outside**, **Inside**, or **Middle** of the object's bounding box.

6. Set other properties as needed:

    ● To vary the border width, select or type a value in the **Weight** list.

    ● If **Behind contents** is checked, the inner half of the border extends behind the object. If unchecked, the whole border appears in front (the wider the border, the more it encroaches on the filled region).

    ● If **Scale with object** is checked, both border and object change together when you resize the object. If unchecked, the border weight remains constant during resizing.

7. Click **OK** when you're done.

Hyperlinking an object

Hyperlinking an object such as a box or Quick Button, a word, or a picture means that a reader of your PDF (or visitor to your Web site) can click on the object to trigger an event. The event might be a jump to a different page, the appearance of an email composition window, the display of a graphic, text, or media file, or a jump to an anchor attached to a target object.

To hyperlink an object:

1. Use the **Pointer Tool** to highlight the region of text, or select an object.

2. Click the 🔗 **Hyperlink** button on the Standard toolbar.

3. In the **Hyperlinks** dialog, click to select the link destination type, and enter the specific hyperlink target—an Internet page, a page in your publication/Web site, an email address, local file, or an object's anchor.

4. Click **OK**.

As a visual cue, hyperlinked words are underlined and appear in the colour you've specified in the Scheme Manager.

> If you're hyperlinking to an object's anchor you'll have to create the anchor in advance of creating a hyperlink. (See Creating a PDF bookmark list on p. 214).

To modify or remove a hyperlink:

1. Use the **Pointer Tool** to select the object, or click for an insertion point inside the linked text. (It's not necessary to drag over a hyperlinked region of text.)

2. Click the **Hyperlink** button on the Standard toolbar, or choose **Hyperlink...** from the Insert menu. The **Hyperlinks** dialog opens with the current link target shown. If the link is in text, the whole text link highlights.

   - To modify the hyperlink, select a new link destination type and/or target.

   - To remove the hyperlink, click the **Remove** button.

> Removing a hyperlink does not remove the underlying object or text.

Working
with Text

Importing text from a file

Importing text from a word-processor file is the traditional way to create text content for Desktop Publishing layouts (but you can also create a story using WritePlus). If you use your current word processor (such as Microsoft Word) to create the text file for your publication, you can import any number of files into one publication. Each file becomes a **story** consisting of a self-contained section of text like a single article in a newspaper, which resides in one or more linked **text frames**.

 PagePlus will preserve the formatting of imported word-processor text. However, if you're using your word processor to create text specifically for PagePlus, you'll save time by typing as text only, and applying formatting later in PagePlus.

To import text from a file:

1. (Optional) If using an existing empty text frame, select the frame. If inserting text into a populated text frame, click for an insertion point (or select a portion of text to be replaced).

2. Choose **Text File...** from the Insert menu.

3. From the **Open** dialog, locate and select the file to import.

4. Check the **Retain Format** box to retain the source file's formatting styles. Uncheck the box to discard this information. In either case, PagePlus will preserve basic character properties like italic, bold, and underline, and paragraph properties like alignment (left, centre, right).

5. Check the **Ignore line wrapping** box to ignore returns in the source text—that is, only if the file has been saved with a carriage return at the end of every line, and you want to strip off these extra returns. Otherwise, leave the box unchecked.

6. Click **Open.** The text will imported into the pre-selected text object or a new text frame.

Understanding text frames

Typically, text in PagePlus goes into **text frames**, which work equally well as containers for single words, standalone paragraphs, or multipage articles or chapter text. You can also use artistic text (see p. 85) for standalone text with special effects, or **table text** (see Creating text-based tables on p. 122) for row-and-column displays.

What's a text frame?

A text frame is effectively a mini-page, with:

- Margins and column guides to control text flow.

- Optional preceding and following frames.

- Text and optional inline images that flow through the frame (from the previous frame and on to the next).

The text in a frame is called a **story**.

- When you move a text frame, its story text moves with it.

- When you resize a text frame, its story text reflows to the new dimensions.

Frames can be linked so that a single story continues from one frame to another. But text frames can just as easily stand alone. Thus in any publication, you can create text in a single frame, spread a story over several frames, and/or include many independent frame sequences. By placing text frames anywhere, in any order, you can build up newspaper or newsletter style publications with a story flowing from one column to another (below) or even across pages.

When you select a frame you'll see its bounding box, indicated by a grey border line plus corner and edge handles, and (if you clicked with the Pointer Tool) a blinking insertion point in the frame's text. In this mode, you can edit the text with the Pointer Tool. As in a word processor, double-clicking selects a word, and triple-clicking selects a paragraph. (For details, see Editing text on the page on p. 92.)

Text frames behave like other PagePlus objects—when selected, you can manipulate them as for shapes, lines, artistic text, and tables. Here's a breakdown of text frame capabilities.

Feature	Supported
Margins and column guides	✓
Breaks (column, page, and frame)	✓
Resize/move frame	✓
Crop frame	✓
Rotate frame	✓[1]
Frame linking	✓
Columns	✓
Export as text	✓
Line attributes	✓
Solid fill and line colour	✓
Gradient and bitmap fill	✓
Transparency	✓[1]
Borders	✓[1]
Warp	✓[1]
2D/3D Filter Effects	✓[1]
Instant 3D	✓[1]

[1] If applied, will export frame as a graphic (Web Publishing mode only).

To select only the frame (no insertion point):

- Click the frame's bounding box.

To move a text frame:

- Drag the frame's bounding box.

To resize a text frame:

- In any selection mode, drag a corner or edge handle.

Creating text frames

You add frames to a page as you would any other object. PagePlus supports a wide variety of frame shapes. You can resize any frame, but cannot alter its basic shape.

To create a frame:

1. Select a text frame from the ![icon] **Text Frame** flyout on the Tools toolbar.
2. Click on the page or pasteboard to create a new frame at a default size.
   OR
   Drag out to place the text frame at your chosen dimensions.

To create a frame (from a shape):

- You can also draw a shape and select **Convert to>Shaped Text Frame** on the Tools menu (text is not auto-aligned).
  OR
  Type directly onto any shape to automatically create a shaped frame (text is automatically centred vertically and horizontally). Useful for creating objects for diagrams!

To delete a frame:

- Select the frame—click its edge until a grey border appears—and then press the **Delete** key.

Putting text into a frame

You can put text into a frame using one of the following methods:

WritePlus story editor:	Click the [A̲I̲] **WritePlus** button on the Frame context toolbar.
	This opens the PagePlus integrated story editor—useful for typing, formatting, and proofing large amounts of text. If the frame already contains text, it is automatically loaded into WritePlus for editing.
Importing text:	Right-click on a frame and choose **Insert Text File...** (shortcut **Ctrl+T**) to import text.
Typing into the frame:	Select the Pointer Tool, then click for an insertion point to type text straight into a frame, or edit existing text. (See Editing text on the page on p. 92.)
Pasting via the Clipboard:	Select the Pointer Tool and click for an insertion point in the text, then press **Ctrl+V**.
Drag and drop:	Select text (e.g. in a word processor file), then drag it onto the PagePlus page. If you drop onto a selected frame, the text is pasted inline after existing text. Otherwise, a new frame is created for the text.

> For testing purposes only, when designing your frame layout, use **Fill with Placeholder Text** on the Insert menu to populate frames with text.

Frame setup and layout

The **frame layout** controls how text will flow in the frame. The frame can contain multiple **columns**. When a frame is selected (and the Frames option is switched on in the View menu), its column margins appear as dashed grey guide lines if set in Frame Setup. Note that unlike the page margin and row/column guides, which serve as layout guides for placing page elements, the frame column guides actually determine how text flows within each frame. Text won't flow outside the column margins.

You can drag the column guides or use a dialog to adjust the top and bottom **column blinds** and the left and right **column margins**.

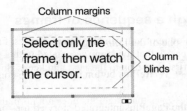

Column margins

Select only the frame, then watch the cursor.

Column blinds

To edit frame properties directly:

- Select the frame object, then drag column guide lines to adjust the boundaries of the column.

(1)   *(2)*   *(3)*

The illustration above shows how the cursor will change when hovering over the bounding box with **Ctrl** key pressed (1), after dragging inwards the column margin can be adjusted (2), and after dragging downwards, the top margin blind can be moved (3).

To edit frame properties using a dialog:

1. Select the frame and click the ⬛ **Frame Setup** button on the Frame context toolbar.

2. From the dialog, you can change the **Number of columns**, **Gutter** distance between columns, **Left Margin**, **Right Margin**, and enable/disable text wrapping around an object.

3. To change the column widths and blinds (top and bottom frame margins), click a cell in the table and enter a new value.

How a story flows through a sequence of frames

You can have just one frame on its own, or you can have many frames. Frames can be connected in linked **sequences** so that the **story** associated with a given frame sequence flows through the first frame on to the next and keeps flowing into frames in the link sequence.

A key difference from a word processor is that PagePlus does not normally add or remove frames according to the amount of text. The text simply flows until the text runs out (and some frames are left empty), or the frames run out (and some text is left over), i.e.

- If the text runs out before the last frame, you have some empty frames. These frames will be filled with text if you add more text to the story, or if you increase the size of the story text.

- If there is still more text to go after filling the last frame, PagePlus stores it in an invisible **overflow area**, remembering that it's part of the story text. If you later add more frames or reduce the size of text in a frame, the rest of the story text is flowed in.

PagePlus keeps track of multiple linked frame sequences, and lets you flow several stories in the same publication. The **Text Manager** (accessed via the Tools menu) provides an overview of all stories and lets you choose which one you want to edit.

On text overflow, the frame's ⊞ AutoFlow button can be used to create new frames for the overflowed text. To control how the frame text is spread throughout available frames, you can use Fit Text, Enlarge Text, or Shrink Text. These options scale a story's text size. See Fitting text to the frames on p. 81.

Fitting text to frames

Fitting story text precisely into a sequence of frames is part of the art of laying out publications.

If there's too much story text to fit in a frame sequence, PagePlus stores it in an invisible **overflow area** and the Link button on the last frame of the sequence displays ⊡; an ⊞ **AutoFlow** button appears next to the Link button. You might edit the story down or make more room for it by adding an extra frame or two to the sequence. Clicking the AutoFlow button adds additional frames and pages as needed (see below).

Once frames are in position it's still possible to control how text is distributed throughout the frame(s) via tools on the Frame context toolbar.

The **Text Sizing** flyout offers three tools for controlling how frame text scales through the text frame. These are "once-off" operations (compared to the "continuous" Autofit Options shown below)

 Fit Text

Click to scale the story's text size so it fits exactly into the available frame(s); further text added to the frame will cause text overflow. You can use this early on, to gauge how the story fits, or near the end, to apply the finishing touch. Fit Text first applies small point size changes, then small leading changes, then adjustments to the paragraph space below value, until the text fits.

 Enlarge Text

Click to increase the story's text size one increment.

 Shrink Text

Click to reduce the story's text size one increment.

Each frame's story text can adopt its own individual autofit settings as follows:

The **AutoFit Options** flyout offers three autofit modes which continuously act upon a selected frame's story text.

 No Autofit

This is the normal mode of operation where, if enabled, text won't automatically scale throughout the selected text frame, possibly leaving partly empty frames at the end of the frame sequence.

 Shrink Text on Overflow

If enabled, as extra text is added to the text frame, all frame text will shrink accordingly to avoid text overflow.

 Autofit

If enabled, the frame will always scale text automatically by adjusting text size (compare to Fit Text which fits text once, with any additional text causing text overflow).

AutoFlow

When importing text, it's a good idea to take advantage of the **AutoFlow** feature, which will automatically create text frames and pages until all the text has been imported. This way, enough frames are created to display the whole story. Then you can gauge just how much adjustment will be needed to fit the story to the available "real estate" in your publication.

If you add more text to a story while editing, or have reduced the size of frame, you may find that an overflow condition crops up. In this case you can decide whether to use AutoFit or click the frame's **AutoFlow** button.

To AutoFlow story text on the page:

- Click the ⊞ **AutoFlow** button just to the left of the frame's ⊡ **Link** button.

PagePlus creates additional pages and frames as needed to accommodate the story text.

Linking text frames

When a text frame is selected, the frame includes a **Link** button at the bottom right which denotes the state of the frame and its story text, and which allows you to control how the frame's story flows to following frames:

⊡ **No Overflow**
    The frame is not linked to a following frame (it's either a standalone frame or the last frame in a sequence) and the frame is empty or the end of the story text is visible.

⊡ **Overflow**
    The frame is not linked (either standalone or last frame) and there is additional story text in the overflow area. An ⊞ **Autoflow** button also appears to the left of the **Link** button.

⊡ **Continued**
    The frame is linked to a following frame. The end of the story text may be visible, or it may flow into the following frame.
    Note: The button icon will be red if the final frame of the sequence is overflowing, or green if there's no overflow.

There are two basic ways to set up a linked sequence of frames:

- You can link a sequence of empty frames, then import the text.

- You can import the text into a single frame, then create and link additional frames into which the text automatically flows.

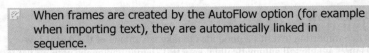

When frames are created by the AutoFlow option (for example when importing text), they are automatically linked in sequence.

To create a link or reorder the links between existing frames, you can use the **Link** button or the controls on the Frame context toolbar. Remember to watch the cursor, which changes to indicate these operations.

To link the selected frame to another frame as the next frame:

- Click the frame's **Link** button (showing ▭.)
  OR

  Select the frame, then click the 🔗 **Link Frame** button on the Frame context toolbar.

- Click with the Textflow cursor on the frame to be linked to. Only empty frames are valid frames to link to.

To unlink the selected frame from the sequence:

- Click the ⬚ **Unlink Frame** button on the Frame context toolbar.
  OR
  Click on the frame's **Link** button, then click with the Textflow cursor on the same frame.

Story text remains with the "old" frames. For example, if you detach the second frame of a three-frame sequence, the story text remains in the first and third frames, which are now linked into a two-frame story. The detached frame is always empty.

To navigate from frame to frame:

- Click the 📄 **Previous Frame** or 📄 **Next Frame** button on the Frame context toolbar.

Using artistic text

Artistic text is standalone text you type directly onto a page. Especially useful for headlines, pull quotes, and other special-purpose text, it's easily formatted with the standard text tools.

ABCDEF

Here are some similarities between frame text and artistic text. Both text types let you:

- vary character and paragraph properties, apply named text styles, edit text in WritePlus and even import text.

- apply different line styles, fills (including gradient and bitmap fills), and transparency.

- access text via the Text Manager.

- track font usage with the Resource Manager.

- embed inline images.

- apply filter effects and rotate/flip.

- use proofing options such as AutoSpell/Spell Checker, Proof Reader, and Thesaurus.

And some differences...

- You can initially "draw" artistic text at a desired point size, and drag it to adjust the size later. Frame text reflows in its frame upon frame resize (but doesn't alter its text size).

- Artistic text can be applied to a path but frame text cannot.

- Artistic text won't automatically line wrap like frame text.

- Artistic text doesn't flow or link the way frame text does; the Frame context toolbar's text-fitting functions aren't applicable to artistic text.

To create artistic text:

1. Choose the **Artistic Text Tool** from the Artistic Text flyout on the Tools toolbar.

2. Click on the page for an insertion point using a default point size, or drag the cross-hair cursor across the page to specify a particular size, e.g.

3. Set initial text properties (font, style, etc.) as needed before typing, using the Text context toolbar, **Format** menu, or right-click (and choose **Text Format>**).

4. Type directly on the page to create the artistic text.

Once you've created an artistic text object, you can select, move, resize, delete, and copy it just as you would with a text frame. Solid colours, gradient/bitmap fills, and transparency can all be applied.

To resize or reproportion an artistic text object:

- To resize while maintaining the object's proportions, drag the resize handles.

- To resize freely, hold down the **Shift** key while dragging.

To edit artistic text:

- Drag to select a range of text; double-click to select a word; or triple-click to select a paragraph.

  Now you can type new text, apply character and paragraph formatting, edit the text in WritePlus, apply proofing options, and so on.

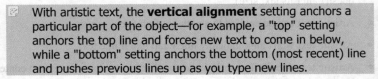

With artistic text, the **vertical alignment** setting anchors a particular part of the object—for example, a "top" setting anchors the top line and forces new text to come in below, while a "bottom" setting anchors the bottom (most recent) line and pushes previous lines up as you type new lines.

Creating logos

Logos are intended to send a clear message to your target audience, all within a simple and identifiable design. Whether you intend to communicate a stylish, business, fun or modern message (below), PagePlus allows you to create impressive logos within a specifically designed and integrated studio environment called **LogoStudio**.

Logos are great for adding to master pages associated with either publications (Paper Publishing mode) or Web sites (Web Publishing mode).

The LogoStudio interface is a lot like PagePlus but its strength is that it allows you to focus on your logo design without the distractions of other objects on the page, i.e. your logo is displayed in isolation. As LogoStudio is an integral part of PagePlus, interworking is mainly transparent and seamless—you can jump between Logo Studio and PagePlus easily and at any time.

LogoStudio comes complete with a range of design templates which can fast-track you to some compelling results. Alternatively, a blank logo can be created or any existing artistic text, shape, gallery object, picture, or grouping thereof within your PagePlus project can be brought into LogoStudio for more detailed logo design work. Each template also offers several layouts based on the chosen template design (e.g., offering different text positions); pick a template and a choice of layouts is made available for selection. Once chosen, a colour set can be adopted.

To create a logo from an existing template:

1. Select 🔲 **Insert Logo** from the Tools toolbar's Logo flyout.

2. From the dialog, pick a design template from the left-hand pane, and then choose your template layout from the right-hand pane. These differ depending on the template chosen.

3. From the upper-right of the dialog, either:

   - To adopt a colour set independent of your document's current colour scheme, keep **Apply colour set** checked and pick a colour set option from the drop-down list.
     OR

   - To adopt the publication's current colour scheme instead, uncheck the **Apply colour set** option.

4. Click **Open**.

5. If your selected logo layout contained text, the displayed dialog will ask for a new **Name** (e.g., company or club name) and, optionally, a tag line (Motto) to personalize the logo. Edit the text and then click **OK**.

6. To insert the logo at a default size, simply click the mouse.
   OR
   To set the size of the logo, drag out a region and release the mouse button.

To create a logo from scratch:

1. Select 🔲 **Insert Logo** from the Tools toolbar's Logo flyout.

2. From the dialog, select the blank thumbnail from the Blank section in the left-hand pane.

3. Click **Open**.

4. To insert the logo at a default size, simply click the mouse to leave a logo placeholder (envelope).
   OR
   To set the size of the logo, drag out the cursor across the page, leaving a placeholder, then release the mouse button.

5. LogoStudio is automaticallly launched from which you can create your custom design using standard tools. Use the supporting LogoStudio help shown in the LogoStudio's user interface if needed.

6. Click ✕ Close LogoStudio from LogoStudio's main toolbar to exit.

Once you've got your template-based logo on the page it's likely that you'll want to modify the logo further. Further objects can be added, or text, filter effects, or fills can be adjusted.

To edit an existing logo:

1. Click the ⊘ button on the control bar under the selected logo.
   LogoStudio is launched with your object(s) zoomed in to fit your workspace.

2. Using standard PagePlus tools and tabs, customize your logo design to your liking.

3. Click ✕ Close LogoStudio from LogoStudio's main toolbar to exit. The modified logo is updated in its original position.

You can use the ⊟ Canvas Setup button to enable a **Fixed Canvas Size** that won't be exceeded. Otherwise, the canvas you work on dynamically resizes as you move objects outside the viewable area. For example, a typical horizontal Web banner of dimensions 468 x 60 pixels could be defined in Web Publishing mode.

The ◇ Canvas Colour ▾ button changes the logo's background colour. Colours from the current Publication Palette, tinted colours from your current colour scheme, or any other colour can be chosen.

Layout Guides can be set via the ▦ Layout Guides button, including Margin Guides and Centre Guides from the Margins tab, and Ruler Guides via the Guides tab. You'll notice that guides are centred on the page by default; the ruler origin is also set to the centre of your workspace.

Converting objects to logos

It's just as easy to by-pass the logo templates and base your design on objects already present in your publication or Web site.

To convert existing objects to a logo:

1. Select one or more objects on the page.

2. Right-click and select **Convert to>**, then pick **Logo...** from the submenu. You can then edit your logo as described above.

OR

1.   Select one or more objects on the page.

2.   Select the  **Edit in LogoStudio** button from the Tools toolbar's Logo flyout.

3.   (Optional) Edit your logo design. In particular, you can use the upper **Logo Text** input box to "caption" your logo (typically a company or club name), then click the green check box.

4.   Click **✕ Close LogoStudio** from the Standard toolbar to exit.

Putting text on a path

"Ordinary" straight-line artistic text is far from ordinary—but you can extend its creative possibilities even further by flowing it along a curved path. The resulting object has all the properties of artistic text, plus its path is a Bézier curve that you can edit with the Pointer Tool as easily as any other line! In addition, text on a path is editable in some unique ways, as described below.

To apply a preset curved path to text:

1.   Create an artistic text object.

2.   With the text selected, on the Text context toolbar, click the ✗ ▾ Path flyout and choose a preset path.

The text now flows along the specified path.

To add artistic text along an existing line or shape:

1. Create a freehand, straight, or curved line (see Drawing and editing lines on p. 163) or a shape (see Drawing and editing shapes on p. 169).

2. Choose the **A** **Artistic Text Tool** from the Artistic Text flyout on the Tools toolbar.

3. Bring the cursor very close to the line. When the cursor changes to include a curve, click the mouse where you want the text to begin.

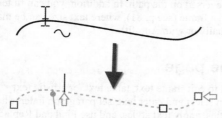

4. Begin typing at the insertion point. Text flows along the line, which has been converted to a path.

To fit existing text to an existing line or shape:

1. Create an artistic text object.

2. Create a freehand, straight, or curved line or a shape.

3. Select both objects. On the **Tools** menu, choose **Fit Text to Curve** from the Tools menu. The text now flows along the specified path.

To create text and path at the same time:

1. Choose one of the Path Text tools from the Text flyout:

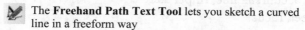

The **Freehand Path Text Tool** lets you sketch a curved line in a freeform way

The **Straight Path Text Tool** is for drawing a straight line

The **Curved Path Text Tool** lets you join a series of line segments (which may be curved or straight) using "connect the dots" mouse clicks

2. Create a line on the page. Your line appears as a path with an insertion point at its starting end (for a curved path you can either type directly onto any part of the path or press **Esc** or double-click to get the insertion point at the start of the path).

3. Begin typing at the insertion point. Text flows along the path.

Artistic text can also be moved along its path, adjusted with respect to text baseline height, and flipping/reversed on the path. See PagePlus help for more details.

Artistic text can also be moved along its path, adjusted with respect to text baseline height, and flipped/reversed on the path. In addition, you can fit text to a path as you would fit text to a frame (see p. 81), where text size can be made to adjust to path length (manually or with Autofit).

Editing text on the page

You can use the Pointer Tool to edit frame text, table text, or artistic text directly. On the page, you can select and enter text, set paragraph indents and tab stops, change text properties, apply text styles, and use Find and Replace. For editing longer stories, and for more advanced options, choose WritePlus (**Edit Story...** from the Edit menu).

Selecting and entering text

The selection of frame text, artistic text, and table text follows the conventions of the most up-to-date word-processing tools. The selection area is shaded in semi-transparent blue for clear editing.

> Nulla vestibulum eleifend
> nulla. Suspendisse potenti.
> Aliquam turpis nisi, venenatis
> non, accumsan nec, imperdiet
> laoreet, lacus.

Double- or triple-click selects a word or paragraph, respectively. You can also make use of the **Ctrl**-click or drag for selection of non-adjacent words, the **Shift** key for ranges of text.

To edit text on the page:

1. Select the Pointer Tool, then click (or drag) in the text object. A standard insertion point appears at the click position (see below).
    OR
    Select a single word, paragraph or portion of text is already selected.

2. Type to insert new text or overwrite selected text, respectively.

Nulla |vestibulum eleifend
nulla. Suspendisse potenti.
Aliquam turpis nisi, venenatis
non, accumsan nec, imperdiet
laoreet, lacus.

To start a new paragraph:

- Press **Enter**.

To start a new line within the same paragraph (using a "line break" or "soft return"):

- Press **Shift+Enter**.

The following two options apply only to frame text. You can use these shortcuts or choose the items from the **Insert>Break** submenu.

To flow text to the next column (Column Break), frame (Frame Break) or page (Page Break):

- Press **Ctrl+Enter**, **Alt+Enter** or **Ctrl+Shift+Enter**, respectively.

To switch between insert mode and overwrite mode:

- Press the **Insert** key.

To repeat a text action:

- Choose **Repeat** from the Edit menu, or press **Ctrl+Y**.

For example, if you've applied new formatting to one paragraph, you can click in another paragraph and use the **Repeat** command to apply the same formatting there.

Copying, pasting and moving text

You can easily copy frame text and paste into the same or a different text frame. Text stored on the clipboard can additionally be pasted into a new frame. Drag and drop support for frame text allows text to be moved into a different location within the same frame or a different text frame in your publication.

To copy and paste text:

1. Select the text to be copied.
2. Select **Copy** from the Edit menu. This places the text onto the clipboard.

3. Place an insertion point in a different location in your story or artistic text.

4. Select **Paste** from the Edit menu.

> If you don't place an insertion point, the text can be pasted into a new text frame directly.

To move text by drag and drop (text frames only):

1. Select the text to be moved.

2. Hover over the selected text and hold your mouse button down. A cursor is shown.

3. Move the cursor to the location (in the same or different frame) you wish to place the text—an insertion point should be displayed.

4. Release the mouse button to place your text.

Setting paragraph indents

When a text object is selected, markers on the horizontal ruler indicate the left indent, first line indent, and right indent of the current paragraph. You can adjust the markers to set paragraph indents, or use a dialog.

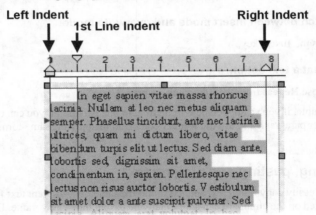

- The **Left** indent is set in relation to the object's left margin.

- The **1st line** indent is in relation to the left indent.

- The **Right** indent is in relation to the object's right margin.

For details on setting frame margins, see Frame setup and layout (on p. 79).

To set the indents of the current paragraph:

- Drag the appropriate ruler marker(s).
  OR

- For quick left indents, select the 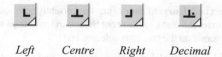 **Increase Level** or **Decrease Level** button to increase or decrease indent, respectively. Indent is by the currently set default tab stop distance.
  OR

- To adjust indent settings numerically, choose **Paragraph...** from the Format menu (or **Text Format>Paragraph...** from the right-click menu). In the Indentation box, you can enter values for Left, Right, 1st Line, or Hanging indents.

Setting tab stops

To set a tab stop:

1. Select the paragraph(s) in which you want to set tab stops.

2. Click the ruler intersection button until it changes to the type of tab you want: (Left, Centre, Right, or Decimal).

⌊	⌊	⌋	⌊
Left	*Centre*	*Right*	*Decimal*

3. Click on the horizontal ruler where you want to set a tab stop. You'll see your tab stop appear.

   - To move a tab stop, drag it to a new ruler position.

   - To delete a tab stop, drag it off the ruler.

> If you want to set precise measurements for tabs, right-click the frame and choose **Text Format**, then select **Tabs...** from the submenu.

Working with Unicode text

PagePlus fully supports Unicode, making it possible to incorporate foreign characters or special symbols.

- To paste Unicode text from the Clipboard to the page, use **Edit>Paste Special...**, then select "Unformatted Unicode Text."

- Insert Unicode characters directly into your text by typing your Unicode Hex value and pressing **Alt+X**. The Alt+X keyboard operation toggles between the displayed character (e.g., @) and its Hex value (e.g., U+0040) equivalent.

- To export text in Unicode format, use WritePlus.

Using Find and Replace

You can search publication text for an extraordinary variety of items: not just words or parts of words, but a host of character and paragraph attributes such as fonts, styles, alignment, bullets and numbering, missing fonts, drop caps... even inline graphics and more! Using the Find and Replace dialog—which remains open without interrupting your work until you click its **Close** button—you can replace globally, or on a case-by-case basis.

To use Find and Replace on frame text:

1. Choose **Find & Replace...** from the Edit menu.

2. In the dialog, type the text to be found in the **Find** box and its replacement text (if any) in the **Replace** box. Click the down arrows to view recent items. Click either box's button to use flyout menus to select formats or special characters, or define a regular expression (for a wildcard-type search).

3. Select the Range to be searched: **Current Story** (just the currently selected text object or story), or **All Stories** (all text), or **Current Selection** (only used with the Replace All function to operate on the currently selected text).

4. Select **Match whole word only** to match character sequences that have white space (space, tab character, page break, etc.) or punctuation at each end, or which are at the start/end of a paragraph. Select **Match case** for case-sensitive search. Select **Regular expressions** to treat the contents of the Find box as an expression, rather than as a literal string to be found.

5. Click **Find Next** to locate the first instance of the Find text.
   OR
   Click **Select All** to highlight all instances of matching text in your document simultaneously.

6. Click **Replace** if you want to substitute with replacement text. Alternatively, click **Find Next** again to skip to the next matching text. Continue using the Replace option as required until you reach the end of your document.
   OR
   Click **Replace All** to replace all instances of the found text with the replacement text at the same time. PagePlus reports when the search is completed.

7. Click **Close** to dismiss the Find and Replace dialog.

The Find and Replace dialog also lets you perform a wildcard-type search by using a **regular expression**—a formula for generating a set of strings—to specify complex search criteria. This is covered in more detail in PagePlus Help.

Inserting footnotes and endnotes

Within frame text, it's easy to add **footnotes** (which normally go at the bottom of a column) and/or **endnotes** (normally at the end of a text story). In either case you can customize the consecutive numbering or symbols used by reference marks, the style of both marks and note body text, and the placement and layout of note text, including optional line separators. You can add and view notes either on the page or in WritePlus.

To insert a footnote or endnote:

1. Click for an insertion point in a text frame. If updating an existing custom mark, select it first.

2. Choose **Footnote/Endnote...** from the Insert menu.

3. Select either the **Footnotes** or **Endnotes** tab.

4. Set the **Number format**, **Start at**, **Restart each**, and **Note position** fields as appropriate.

PagePlus displays the new footnote/endnote followed by a text edit cursor, so you can immediately enter the text of the note.

Setting text properties

PagePlus gives you a high degree of typographic control over characters and paragraphs, whether you're working with frame text, table text, or artistic text.

To apply basic text formatting:

1. Select the text.

2. Use buttons on the Text context toolbar to change text style, typeface, point size, attributes, paragraph alignment, or level.

> If a font is unavailable and has been substituted (see p. 100), its font name on the Context toolbar is prefixed by the "?" character.

To clear local formatting:

- Select a range of text with local formatting.

- Click on the **Clear Formatting** option on the Text context toolbar's text styles drop-down list (or Text Styles tab).

Using fonts

One of the most dramatic ways to change your document's appearance is to change the fonts used in your artistic text, frame text, or table text. Applying different fonts to a character or entire paragraph can communicate very different messages to your intended readership.

Lorem Ipsum

LOREM IPSUM

Lorem Ipsum *Lorem Ipsum*

Lorem Ipsum

Font assignment is very simple in PagePlus, and can be done from the Fonts tab, Text context toolbar, or in the **Character** dialog (via right-click, or from the Format menu). The Fonts tab lets you:

- Apply fonts easily without dialog navigation.

- Assign fonts to be Websafe or favourites.

- View most recently used, Websafe, and your favourite fonts simultaneously.

- Search for installed fonts via search box.

- Hover-over preview of fonts applied to your document's text (optional).

- Change a font for another throughout your Publication or Web site (by right-click Select All).

- Access Serif FontManager (subject to availability).

The **Fonts** tab is automatically hidden by default, but can be viewed by clicking the arrow button at the left of your workspace. You may also need to click the **Fonts** label to display the **Fonts** tab.

Assigning and previewing fonts

The fonts shown in the **Fonts** tab represent the currently installed fonts on your computer. This means that these fonts are available to format any selected character or paragraph.

To assign a font:

- Select some text, then click on the font name in the Fonts tab to assign the font to the text.

You can preview how fonts will appear on your selected text by enabling PagePlus's font preview feature.

To preview fonts:

1. From the tab's ▶ **Tab Menu** button (top-right of tab), check the **Preview Font** option.

2. Select a section of text (a letter, word, or paragraph) in your document.

3. On the **Fonts** tab, hover over any font in the list. The selected text will update to show how the font will appear in situ.

4. (Optional) Click on the font in the Fonts tab to assign the font to the text.

Changing common fonts

Changing one font for another is very simple for a single portion of text, but the **Fonts** tab can take things a step a further by allowing a font to be located throughout the entire document, and if necessary, swapped for another font. It's simple to then re-assign a different font to the selected text.

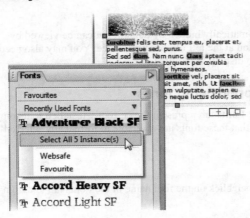

To select (and change) a font throughout your document:

1. Right-click a font displayed in the **Fonts** tab.

   If the font is used in your document, you'll see a "*Select All n instance(s)*" message (*n* is the number of times the font is used). If there are no occurrences, you'll get a "*Not currently used*" message.

2. Click the message label, making it shaded in blue—text formatted with the chosen font is selected.

3. Hover over font names in your font list. Click on a chosen font to apply it to the selected text.

Substituting fonts

Font substitution issues may arise when opening PagePlus Publications (*.PPP) and importing PDF files that have no embedded fonts. This is because the fonts used in the original document may not be present on the target PC. If this occurs, font substitution of that unavailable font will be indicated to the user via a dialog as the PPP or PDF file is opened—the font status will be "Not Available".

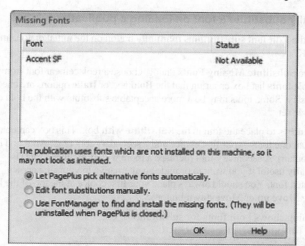

PagePlus's font substitution mechanism makes use of the PANOSE Font Matching System which intelligently finds the best font substitution match between a missing and a locally available font. By default, clicking **OK** will substitute the missing font for a locally available standard font (e.g., Arial) automatically. Optionally, you can manually substitute the missing font with the font of your choosing by enabling the **Edit font substitutions manually** button instead.

A third option, is to use Serif's FontManager program which can search and load uninstalled fonts if located (fonts are uninstalled after use). See Using FontManager on p. 104.

> To avoid font substitution, try to source original fonts from the originating PC if possible.
>
> PagePlus will use any embedded TrueType (TTF) fonts and OpenType fonts with TTF or Type 1 outlines in imported PDF to honour the intended appearance of imported text that uses those fonts.

To manually substitute a font on loading a publication:

1. Enable the **Edit font substitutions manually** button on the initial dialog, and click **OK**.

2. From the **Substitute Missing Fonts** dialog, choose a replacement font from the **Available fonts** list box ensuring that the **Bold** and/or **Italic** options are checked if necessary. Some fonts may be a more acceptable substitute with the bold or italic style set.

3. Click **Add<<** to place the font in the **Substitute with** box. This box can contain more than one font—your first choice and a secondary font (e.g., Arial or Times New Roman). A secondary font (perhaps a more widely available font) is particularly useful if you want to provide an alternative to your first choice substituted font. You should always place your first choice at the top of the list with the **Move up** or **Move down** buttons.

   The dialog shows both fonts for substitutions, e.g.

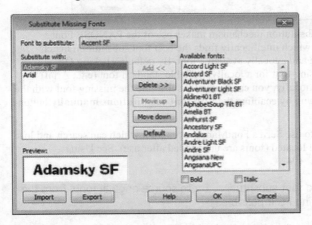

The Adamsky SF font is first choice, with Arial used as a secondary font.

4. Click **OK**.

> ● Reset the Substitute with box by clicking the Default button. This will replace the fonts listed with a single font, e.g. Arial or Times New Roman, as governed by Windows (this is not configurable).

To manually substitute a font any time:

1. Select **Resource Manager** from the Tools menu.

2. Choose the **Fonts** tab, and click the **Substitutions** button.

3. In the dialog, select the missing font to be substituted from the **Font to substitute** drop-down menu.

4. Carry out font substitution as described in the previous procedure. Repeat for each font to be substituted using the **Font to substitute** drop-down menu.

Clearly, the process of substituting large numbers of fonts is time-consuming, a challenge to the memory and most importantly document specific only. As a solution, especially if the same substitutions need to be applied between different publications in the future, you can export all your font mappings to a single Serif Font Map (*.SFM) file which can subsequently be imported into other publications—saving you the effort of recreating the mappings again. The SFM file replaces the font mapping information stored within the publication.

> The font map file is binary so cannot be edited.

To export Serif Font Map files:

1. Perform font mappings for all missing fonts as described above.

2. Select the **Export** button.

3. Save your font substitutions to a named Serif Font Map (SFM) file in a chosen location.

To import Serif Font Map files:

1. Open a publication to which you want to apply saved font substitutions.

2. Select **Resource Manager** from the Tools menu.

3. Choose the **Fonts** tab, and select the **Substitutions** button.

4. Select the **Import** button.

5. Locate the Serif Font Map (SFM) file, select it and click **Open**.

Saved substitutions in the Font Map file are applied to the current publication.

For PDF imports especially, if you want all new publications to utilize the font substitutions used in your current publication, use the **Tools>Save Defaults** option to make the current font substitutions your default.

Using FontManager

FontManager is a standalone Serif application that works alongside PagePlus with respect to font substitution. Its main feature is to locate and dynamically install a publication's missing fonts. The following procedure assumes FontManager is installed.

 FontManager is a separate application to PagePlus and, as a result, may not be available for sale in your locality.

To install fonts dynamically with FontManager:

1. Launch Serif PagePlus and open a PagePlus publication (*.PPP) OR PDF file.

2. From the dialog, enable the **Use the FontManager...** option (greyed out if FontManager is not installed). This locates and dynamically installs any missing fonts which are currently uninstalled but are present on your PC.

When the current session is closed, the dynamically installed fonts will uninstall automatically.

Using text styles

It's a good idea to establish the main text and graphic formatting to be used in your publication early in the creative process. PagePlus facilitates this by letting you use named **text styles** (pre- or user-defined), which can be applied to frame text, table text, or artistic text. A text style is a set of character and/or paragraph attributes saved as a group. When you apply a style to text, you apply the whole group of attributes in just one step. For example, you could use named paragraph styles for particular layout elements, such as "Heading 1" or "Body," and character styles to convey meaning, such as "Emphasis," "Strong," or "Subtle Reference." Using styles not only speeds the task of laying out a publication but ensures consistency and ease of updating.

Styles can be applied to characters or paragraphs using either the Text context toolbar or the Text Styles tab. Both paragraph and character styles can be managed from the **Text Style Palette**.

Paragraph and character styles

A **paragraph style** is a complete specification for the appearance of a paragraph, including all font and paragraph format attributes. Every paragraph in PagePlus has a paragraph style associated with it.

- PagePlus includes a built-in paragraph style called **"Normal"** with a specification consisting of generic attributes including left-aligned, 12pt Times New Roman. Initially, the "Normal" style is the default for any new paragraph text you type. You can modify the "Normal" style by redefining any of its attributes, and create or adopt any number of new or pre-defined paragraph styles having different names and attributes.

- Applying a paragraph style to text updates all the text in the paragraph except sections that have been locally formatted. For example, a single word marked as bold would remain bold when the paragraph style was updated.

A **character style** includes only font attributes (name, point size, bold, italic, etc.), and you apply it at the character level—that is, to a range of selected characters—rather than to the whole paragraph.

- Typically, a character style applies emphasis (such as italics, bolding or colour) to whatever underlying font the text already uses; the assumption is that you want to keep that underlying font the same. The base character style is shown in the Text Styles tab (or palette) as "Default Paragraph Font, " which has no specified attributes but basically means "whatever font the paragraph style already uses."

- Applying the **Default Paragraph Font** option from the Text Styles tab (or the Text context toolbar's Styles box) will strip any selected local character formatting you've added and will restores original text attributes (paragraph styles are not affected).

- As with paragraph styles, you can define any number of new character styles using different names and attributes (or adopt a pre-defined character style).

Working with named styles

Normal ▾ The named style of the currently selected text is displayed in either the Text Styles tab or the drop-down **Styles** box on the Text context toolbar. A character style (if one is applied locally) may be shown; otherwise it indicates the paragraph style. You can use either the tab, the drop-down Styles box, or a dialog to apply a particular style to the existing text. The Text Style Palette lets you modify an existing style, import styles, or define a new style.

☐ Show All By default, a limited set of styles are shown in the Text Styles tab, although you can display all styles by checking the tab's **Show All** option (or via **Tools>Options>UI Settings**). The Default Paragraph Font, some common styles, and your document's currently used styles (plus any associated styles) will always be shown. You can preview any style and then apply it to a word, paragraph, or story.

To apply a named style:

1. Using the Pointer Tool, click in a paragraph (if applying a paragraph style) or select a range of text (if applying a character style).

2. Display the **Text Styles** tab and select a style from the style list.
   OR
   On the Text context toolbar, click the arrow to expand the Styles drop-down list and select a style name.

The applied style appears in the tab's style list.

To update a named style using the properties of existing text:

1. Make your desired formatting changes to any text that uses a named style.

2. On the **Text Styles** tab, right-click the style and choose **Update <style> to Match Selection**.
   OR
   On the Text context toolbar, click the arrow to expand the Styles drop-down list and select the current style name again. Click **OK** to confirm the option to "Update the style to reflect recent changes."

All text using the named style, throughout the publication, takes on the new properties.

To create a new style:

1. Either:
   1. On the **Text Styles** tab, select the style on which you want your new style to be based.

   2. Click the ⬛ **Create Style** button, or right-click and choose **Base New Style on** <*selected style name*>.

      OR

      - Choose **Text Style Palette...** in the Format menu, and with a "base" style selected in the dialog, click the **Create...** button.

2. In the **Text Style** dialog, define the style **Name**, the style to be **Based on**, **Style for the following paragraph**, and the style to be changed to if Increase Level is applied. Check **Always list in Studio** to ensure the style will always appear in the **Text Styles** tab.

3. In the left tree menu change any character or paragraph attributes, tabs, bullets, and drop caps you want to include in the new style definition.

4. Click **OK** to create the style, or **Cancel** to abandon changes.

To create a new style using the properties of existing text:

1. Format the text as desired.

2. To define a character style, select a range of reformatted text. To define a paragraph style, deselect text but leave a blinking cursor (insertion point) within the newly formatted section.

3. Type a new style name into the Text context toolbar's Styles box and press **Enter**.

The new style is defined with the properties of the selected text.

To modify an existing style:

1. From the Text Styles tab:

   - Right-click on the character or paragraph style you want to modify and then choose **Modify <style>...**
     OR

   - With a style selected, pick the **Manage Styles** button from the **Text Styles** tab, then choose the **Modify...** button.

2. From the Text Style dialog, define (or change) the style name, base style, and any character or paragraph attributes, tabs, bullets, and drop caps you want to include in the style definition.

3. Click **OK** to accept style properties, or **Cancel** to abandon changes.

4. Click **Apply** to update text, or click **Close** to maintain the style in the site for future use.

Alternatively, choose **Text Style Palette...** from the Format menu to modify styles.

Removing local formatting

To return characters and/or paragraphs back to their original formatting, click on the **Clear Formatting** option in the Text Styles tab. This is great for reverting some formatting which hasn't quite worked out! You can clear the formatting of selected characters, paragraphs, or both depending on what text is currently selected. The following table indicates the effects of different types of text selection on clear formatting.

Selection	Clicking Clear Formatting affects..
Word	Character
Range of text	Character
Single paragraph	Character and Paragraph
Multiple paragraphs	Paragraph
Story text	Character and Paragraph
Text frame	Character and Paragraph

You also have the flexibility to be more explicit about how clear formatting is applied by clicking on the Clear Formatting option's drop-down arrow, i.e.

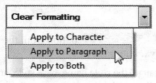

To remove local formatting:

1. Select locally formatted characters or paragraph(s) as described in the above table.

2. Either:

   - Select **Clear Formatting** from the **Styles** drop-down list on the Text context toolbar.
     OR
     On the **Text Styles** tab, click the **Clear Formatting** option.
     OR
     From the same tab, select **Apply to Both** from the drop-down menu or **Clear Text Formatting** from the Format menu).
     OR
     Select **Apply to Character** to remove all local character formatting (leaving paragraph formatting untouched).
     OR
     Select **Apply to Paragraph** to remove all local paragraph formatting (leaving character formatting untouched).

Like **Clear Formatting**, you can use **Reapply Styles** on the **Text Styles** tab (or Text context toolbar) to clear all local overrides leaving the default text. However, where Clear Formatting reverts the text to Normal style, Reapply styles reverts the text back to its current name style. Use **Apply to Character** (retaining paragraph styles overrides), **Apply to Paragraph** (retaining character style overrides), and **Apply to Both** to remove both character or paragraph style overrides simultaneously.

If you prefer, you can remove a style's formatting, enabling you to start building up your text style again. Choose **Manage Styles** button on the Text Styles tab, click the **Modify** button, then click the **Clear All** button from the General section.

Changing common styles

Changing one character or paragraph style for another is very simple for a single portion of text. However, in PagePlus, it's just as easy to swap one style for another by selecting multiple instances of the style and choosing an alternative style. This swaps styles across paragraphs and throughout entire stories all at the same time.

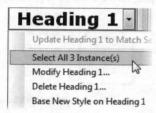

To select (and change) a style throughout your document:

1. Right-click a style displayed on the **Text Styles** tab.

2. If the style is used in your document, you'll see a "*Select All n instance(s)*" message (*n* is the number of times the style is used).

   If there are no occurrences of the style, you'll see a "*Not currently used*" message.

3. Click the message label—text formatted with the chosen style is highlighted.

4. Hover over style names in your styles list, then click on a chosen style to apply the style to the selected text.

Wrapping text

PagePlus lets you wrap frame text around the contours of a separate object. Usually, this means wrapping text to a picture that overlaps or sits above a text frame. But you can wrap frame text around a shape, artistic text, table, or another frame. Wrapping is accomplished by changing the **wrap setting** for the object to which text will wrap.

To wrap text around an object:

1. Select the object around which you want the text to wrap.

2. Click the ▣ **Wrap Settings** button on the Arrange toolbar.

3. Select the manner in which text will wrap around the object by clicking a sample, i.e.

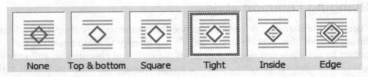

| None | Top & bottom | Square | Tight | Inside | Edge |

4. Choose which side(s) the chosen wrapping method will be applied, again by clicking a sample.

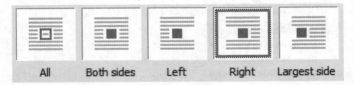

| All | Both sides | Left | Right | Largest side |

The examples show tight wrapping applies to the right of the object only.

5. Click **OK**.

In addition, you can specify the **Distance from text**: the "standoff" between the object's **wrap outline** and adjacent text. (The wrap outline is a contour that defines the object's edges for text wrapping purposes.) Different object types have different initial wrap outlines. For QuickShapes, the wrap outline corresponds exactly to the object's edges, while for closed shapes the outline is a rectangle.

You can manually adjust the wrap outline using the Curve context toolbar for more precise text fitting. See PagePlus help for more information.

Flowing text around inline images

An "inline" image is one you've imported at an insertion point in a text object, or have pasted into a text object. (Where text flow is concerned, inline picture frames behave just like inline images.) Both frame and artistic text will flow around an inline image if the picture's alignment setting is Left, Centre, Right, or Indent (shown below), but not if it's Top, Middle, or Bottom (shown below).

You can also adjust the Distance from text, which (as with regular text wrap) affects the "standoff" between the object and adjacent text.

With frame text, the effect is similar to wrapping around a separate object, as detailed above. Lines of artistic text, on the other hand, are only terminated by line breaks and don't wrap—rather they break around the image and the text object expands to the right.

To flow text around an inline image or picture frame:

1. Right-click the inline image or frame.

2. Use the **Align** flyout to set **Left**, **Centre**, **Right**, or **Indent**.
   OR
   Choose **Properties...** from the menu. In the **Picture Properties** dialog, set the **Align** type. Optionally, set the **Distance from text**, i.e. the indent from Left, Right, Top, or Bottom, then click **OK**.

Creating a bulleted or numbered list

You can turn a series of paragraphs into **bulleted**, **numbered** or **multi-level lists**. Bullets are especially useful when listing items of interest in no specific order of preference, numbered lists for presenting step-by-step procedures (by number or letter), and multi-level lists for more intelligent hierarchical lists with prefixed numbers, symbols, or a mix of both, all with supporting optional text (see Using multi-level lists on p. 113).

Bulleted list   *Numbered list*   *Multi-level list*

PagePlus lets you create simple lists directly from the Text context toolbar or choose from a preset bullet, number or multi-level lists via dialog. If you want to go a step further you can create custom list styles by selecting your own symbols, numbers and letter formats. You then have the option of replacing an existing preset with your own preset based on your own custom list style.

Lists can be applied to normal text (as local formatting) or to text styles equally.

To create a simple bulleted or numbered list:

1. Select one or more paragraphs.
   OR
   Click in a paragraph's text.

2. Select **Bulleted list** or **Numbered list** from the Text context toolbar.

   The list style used is the first preset shown in the Bullets & Numbering dialog described below.

To create a bulleted or numbered list (using presets):

1. Select one or more paragraphs.
   OR
   Click in a paragraph's text.

2. Select **Bullets & Numbering...** from the Format menu.

3. From the Text Style dialog, choose **Bullet**, **Number**, or **Multi-Level** from the drop-down menu.

4. Select one of the preset formats shown by default.
   OR
   For a custom list, click the **Details** button to display, then alter custom options.

5. Click **OK** to apply list formatting.

Each time you insert a following return, a new line will begin with the specified symbol or number. In addition, typing two returns in a row (pressing **Enter** twice) cancels bullets or numbers and resumes regular paragraph formatting.

> For number and multi-level lists, check Restart numbering to restart numbering from the current cursor position in the list; otherwise, leave the option unchecked.

To turn off bullets, numbering or multi-level list formatting:

1. Select the paragraph with list formatting.

2. Select **Bullets & Numbering...** from the Format menu.
   OR
   Right-click the paragraph and from the **Text Format** option, choose **Bullets & Numbering...**

3. In the **Text Style** dialog, click the **None** preset option. For custom lists, you may need to click the Preset button first to show the None preset.

Using multi-level lists

For multi-level lists, as opposed to bulleted and numbered lists, you can set a different character (symbol, text or number) to display at each level of your list. Levels are normally considered to be subordinate to each other, where Level 1 (first level), Level 2 (second), Level 3 (third), etc. are of decreasing importance in the list.

1   Vestibulum velit orci,
Nullam sed enim. Dui
   1.1   Lorem ipsum
       pendisse poter
   1.2   Mauris vitae a
       nean arcu elit,
       ligula
       1.2.1   Quisqu
       1.2.2   Donec
           Duis b
           molest
           tum le

2   In hac habitasse plate
Proin mattis eleifend

3   Proin mattis eleifend
pede tellus, dictum eg

For example, the simple multi-level numbered passage of text opposite is arranged at three "nested" levels.

The flexibility of PagePlus's multi-level bullet and numbering system means that you have full control over what gets displayed at each level. For this reason, no common numbering schema needs to exist between levels, i.e. the list could equally be prefixed with a different symbol, text prefix, or number at each level.

If you apply a multi-level preset to a range of text you'll get a list with the preset's Level 1 format applied by default. Unless you use text styles, you'll have to change to levels 2, 3, 4, etc. to set the correct level for your list entry.

Changing list levels on selected paragraphs:

- Click the ⯗ **Increase Level** or ⯗ **Decrease Level** button on the Text context toolbar to increment or decrement the current level by one.

The multi-level presets offer some simple but commonly used schemas for paragraph list formatting. However, if you want to create your own lists or modify an existing list (your own or a preset), PagePlus will do this.

Creating a multi-level list from selected paragraphs:

1. Select **Bullets & Numbering...** from the Format menu.

2. With the **Style** drop-down menu set to Multi-Level, select the list preset called **None**, and click the **Details** button.

3. From the dialog, you can use the **Format** field to build up a list format for the currently selected **Level**. Pick the Level then the **List type**, which could be bulleted, numeric, roman numeric, or alphabetic.

4. Choose a **Start at** value from which the currently set level's sequence will begin.

5. Adjust the character position details including indents (**Number at** and **Text indent**), first tab position (**Tabstop at**), and list **Align** for that level.

6. Repeat the process for each subsequent level needed for the list. You can edit the **Format** structure for each new level if needed.

> Reference another level in your Format field by selection from the **Insert** drop-down list, optionally choosing a font and its attributes via the **Font...** button.

To modify an existing preset, select it from the list and click the **Details** button. Change the list settings as described above and select the **OK** button.

When you create any type of list, whether bulleted, numbered or multi-level, the list's settings can be recalled by reselecting any part of the list and choosing **Bullets & Numbering...** from the Format menu. If a preset was used, PagePlus remembers this and shows the presets page; if the list was a custom list (and not saved as a preset) the Details page is shown. It's possible to save the custom list as a preset at any time.

To save list as new preset:

1. Click anywhere on a custom list, then select **Bullets & Numbering...** from the Format menu to display the Details page.

2. Click the **Preset** button, then pick a preset that you want to overwrite.

3. A dialog prompts you to overwrite the preset, i.e. "*Store current list in preset n?*". Select **Yes** to overwrite the existing preset.

Assigning bullets, numbers, and levels to styles

The lists discussed so far are usually applied as local formatting to a single style, typically "Normal" or "Body". To prove this, you'll see the list structure disappear if you apply **Clear Formatting** (from the Text Styles tab or Text context toolbar's Styles drop-down menu) on the selected list.

If you're working on long documents, there's a fair chance that you'll be using pre-assigned text styles (Heading 1, Heading 2, indent, etc.) to format your document rather than using the above local formatting. You can use such text styles along with list styles to number headings or paragraphs automatically without the need to repetitively format headings or paragraphs as lists. As an example, headings and paragraphs in technical and legal documents are typically prefixed by numbers for easy reference. The advantage of using a style-driven approach is that you can let the numbering take care of itself while you concentrate on applying styling to your document.

If you plan to create your own multi-level paragraph styles, make use of the **Style for Increase Level** option when creating text styles. This sets the paragraph style that will be automatically applied to text if **Increase Level** is applied from the context toolbar; another advantage is that if you apply a multi-level style to text, the associated next level's style will be made available in the Text Styles tab.

PagePlus lets you easily associate any bulleted, numbered or multi-level list style (either preset or custom list) to an existing text style. See Using text styles on p. 104.

Inserting a symbol

You can insert any character from any font installed on your system, using either the Insert menu or (for common symbols) keyboard shortcuts (see PagePlus Help). You can also use a convenient keyboard switch to enter **subscripts** or **superscripts**.

To insert a symbol character:

1. Select the Pointer Tool and click in the text for an insertion point.
2. Choose **Symbol** from the Insert menu, and select a symbol from the submenu.

3. If you need a symbol not shown on the submenu, select **Other...** to display the Insert Symbol dialog. The dialog remains open so you can continue editing in the workspace as you select symbols.

    • Select a **Font** to display its full character set, and then scroll the font table to view characters. You can choose from the **Subset** list to jump to a particular range within the character set.

    • Click any individual character (or select it while browsing using the arrow keys on your keyboard) to view the character's name and Unicode Index at the bottom of the dialog. You can also enter any Unicode hex value and click **Go** to jump to that particular character in the current font.

    • To insert a character into your text, double-click it (or select it and click **Insert**).

To enter subscript or superscript characters:

•   Press **Ctrl+=** to enter subscript mode, or **Ctrl+Shift+=** for superscript mode. Type the subscript or superscript, then press the key combination again to return to entering regular characters.

Inserting date/time

You can insert a date/time field into your text, stamped with current date/time information, by using **Information>Date or Time...** from the Insert menu. Various date and time formats are available. By default, the date/time field updates itself automatically when the publication is saved or loaded. You can turn auto-updating off if necessary.

Inserting user details

When you create a publication from a Design Template for the first time, you may be prompted to update your user details (from a User Details dialog) which will then be used for subsequent design templates. This means you don't need to re-enter the same information the next time it's required in your next Design Template. (Note that some templates don't make use of these user details so a prompt may not occur.)

You can also use this User Details dialog to review your User Details at any time.

Whether opening a template, or updating an existing publication, the fields (once edited) can be updated at the click of a button.

> To switch off prompting for user details, uncheck the **Show when opening new templates** check box in the User Details dialog.

To add, edit or change User Details:

1. Click the **Set User Details** button on the Pages context toolbar (deselect objects to view).

2. Enter new information into the spaces on the **Business**, **Home**, or **Custom** tab (a **Calendars** tab will appear if there is a calendar in your publication).

You can also insert one or more User Details fields into any publication at any time. The **Custom** tab of the User Details dialog includes modifiable and nameable fields into which you can enter any information you may frequently need to "plug into" your publications.

To insert a User Detail field:

1. Select the Pointer Tool and click in the text for an insertion point.

2. Choose **Information** from the Insert menu, then select **User Details...** from the submenu.

3. Select a User Detail entry, and optionally any text **Prefix** or suffix (**Postfix**) to include with your user details, e.g. *Name:*.

4. Click **OK**.

To update fields:

- Enter new information in the User Details dialog (via **Tools>Set User Details...**).

- Click the **Update** button to automatically update any altered field currently placed in your publication or template. This field will remain linked to User Details until it is deleted.

Viewing and changing document information

PagePlus maintains basic properties and statistics for each publication file.

To view or change document properties:

1. Choose **Properties...** from the File menu.

2. Click the **Summary** tab to view or change fields for Author, Keywords, Comments, Title, and Subject.

3. Click the **Statistics** tab to view key dates, last saved information, etc.

To insert document information in your text:

1. Select the Pointer Tool and click in the text for an insertion point.

2. Choose **Information** from the Insert menu, then select **Publication Info...** from the submenu. Select a property to insert and click **OK**.

If the document information changes and **Update automatically** is checked, the document information field in the text is automatically updated when the publication is saved or loaded.

Using AutoCorrect and AutoSpell

PagePlus includes two powerful support tools to nip possible spelling errors in the bud. The **AutoCorrect** feature overcomes common typing errors and lets you build a custom list of letter combinations and substitutions to be applied automatically as you type. You can also turn on **AutoSpell** feature to mark possible problem words in your story text in red. Both features apply to frame text, table text, and artistic text.

If you prefer to address spelling issues in larger doses, at any point along the way you can run the Spell Checker.

AutoCorrect

To set options for automatic text correction:

1. Choose **Options...** from the Tools menu and select the **Auto-Correct** page.

2. Check your desired correction options as required.
   Note: Check **Replace text while typing** to turn on AutoCorrect.

To create a correction list:

1. In the **Replace** field, type a name for the AutoCorrect entry. This is the abbreviation or word to be replaced automatically as you type. For example, if you frequently mistype "product" as "prodcut," type "prodcut" in the Replace box.

2. In the **With** field, type the text to be automatically inserted in place of the abbreviation or word in the **Replace** field.

3. Click the **Add** button to add the new entry to the list.

4. To modify an entry in the correction list, select it in the list, then edit it in the **Replace** and **With** field above. Click the **Replace** button below.

5. To remove an entry, select it and click **Delete**.

To turn off AutoCorrect:

- Uncheck **Replace text while typing**.

AutoSpell

To turn AutoSpell on (or off):

1. Choose **Options...** from the Tools menu.

2. From the General menu option, check (or uncheck) **Autospell**.

When AutoSpell is activated, possible problem words in your story text are marked in red, and you can view a list of suggested alternatives.

To view alternatives:

1. Right-click a marked word.

2. To replace a marked word, choose an alternative spelling from the menu.

3. To tell PagePlus to ignore (leave unmarked) all instances of the marked word in the publication, choose **Ignore All** from the right-click menu.

4. To add the marked word (as spelled) to your personal dictionary, choose **Add to Dictionary** from the right-click menu. This means PagePlus will subsequently ignore the word in any publication.

5. To run the Spelling Checker Wizard, choose **Check Spelling...** from the menu.

Spell-checking

The **Spell Checker** lets you check the spelling of a single word, selected text, a single story, or all stories in your publication. (To help trap spelling errors as they occur, use AutoCorrect and AutoSpell.) You can customize the built-in dictionary by adding your own words.

Multilingual spell checking is supported by use of up to 14 dictionaries. Any language can be enabled globally from **Tools>Options>General** or applied specifically to text or paragraphs via the Language Selector in the Character tab. Spell checking can be turned off temporarily by selecting "None" as a language type—this could be useful when working with text containing lots of unusual terms (perhaps scientific or proprietary terminology).

To check spelling:

1. (Optional) To check a single story, first make sure the text or text object is selected.

2. Choose **Spell Checker...** from the Tools menu.
   OR

   (In WritePlus) Click the abc **Spell Check** button.

3. (Optional) In the dialog, click **Options...** to set preferences for ignoring words in certain categories, such as words containing numbers or domain names.

4. Select **Check currently selected story only** or **Check all stories in my publication** to select the scope of the search.

5. Click **Start** to begin the spelling check.

When a problem is found, PagePlus highlights the problem word. The dialog offers alternative suggestions, and you can choose to **Change** or **Ignore** this instance (or all instances) of the problem word, with the option of adding the problem word to your dictionary.

6. Spell checking continues until you click the **Close** button or the spell-check is completed.

To check the spelling of a single word:

1. With the AutoSpell feature turned on (from **Tools>Options>General**), select in a marked word, then right-click. You'll see alternative spellings on the context menu.

2. To replace the word, choose an alternative spelling from the menu.

3. To tell PagePlus to ignore (leave unmarked) all instances of the marked word in the publication, choose **Ignore All**.

4. To add the marked word (as spelled) to your personal dictionary, choose **Add to Dictionary**. This means PagePlus will ignore the word in any publication.

Automatic proofreading

The **Proof Reader** checks for grammar and readability errors in selected text, a single story, or all text in your publication. You can use Proof Reader from either PagePlus or WritePlus.

To start automatic proofreading:

1. To check a single story, first make sure the text or text object is selected.

2. Choose **Proof Reader...** from the Tools menu.

3. If necessary, click the **Options** button to set options for proofreading, including a spell-check option and the level of formality (with checks for rule types).

4. Select **Check currently selected story only** or **Check all stories in my publication** to select the scope of the search.

5. Click **Start** to begin proof reading.

When a problem is found, PagePlus highlights the problem word. The dialog offers alternative suggestions, and you can choose to **Change** or **Ignore** this instance (or all instances) of the problem word.

6. Proofreading continues until you click the **Close** button or the process is completed.

Using the thesaurus

The **Thesaurus** lets you find synonyms, definitions, and variations of words in your publication text. You can use the Thesaurus from either PagePlus or WritePlus.

To display the Thesaurus:

1. To look up a specific word, first drag to highlight it.

2. Choose **Thesaurus...** from the Tools menu.

3. To look up a different word, type it into the "Replace/Look Up" box and click the **Look Up** button.

If the selected word or word entered is found in the Thesaurus database:

- The "Meanings" list shows definitions for the word in the "Looked Up" box. Initially, the first definition is selected.

- The "Synonyms" list shows synonyms for the definition selected in the "Meanings" box. Initially, the first synonym appears in the "Replace/Look Up" box.

To pop a new word into the "Replace/Look Up" box:

- Click the word in the "Synonyms" list.
  OR
  Type a new word directly into the "Replace/Look Up" box.

You can navigate indefinitely through the thesaurus by selecting the specific meaning, followed by the specific synonym you are interested in and then clicking on the **Look Up** button to get a new range of meanings and synonyms for the new word.

To replace the original word:

- Click the **Replace** button to replace the original word (selected in your text) with the word in the "Replace/Look Up" box.

To exit the thesaurus:

- Click the **Cancel** button.

Creating text-based tables

Tables are ideal for presenting text and data in a variety of easily customizable row-and-column formats, with built-in spreadsheet capabilities.

10	Donec neque	443-X23
2	elementum	432-Y12
2	pellentesque	142-Y08
13	lobortis	133-W33

Each cell in a table behaves like a mini-frame. Like frame text you can vary character and paragraph properties, apply named text styles, embed inline images, apply text colour fills (solid, gradient, or bitmap), track font usage with the Resource Manager, and use proofing options such as AutoSpell/Spell Checker, Proof Reader, and Thesaurus. Some unique features include number formatting and formula insertion.

Feature	Supported
Resize/move table	✓
Rotate table	✓[1]
Rotate table text (in cell)	✓[1]
Sort table contents	✓
Solid fill and border colour	✓
Gradient and bitmap fill	✓
Transparency	✓[1]
Borders	✓[1]

Warp	✓¹
2D/3D Filter effects	✓¹
Instant 3D	✓¹
QuickClear/QuickFill/AutoFormat	✓
Edit cell text in WritePlus	✓
View cell text in Text Manager	✓
Pasting of Excel cell contents	✓

¹ If applied, will export table as a graphic (Web Publishing mode only).

> Table text doesn't flow or link the way frame text does; the Frame context toolbar's text-fitting functions aren't applicable.

To create a table:

1. On the Tools toolbar, choose the **Table Tool** from the Table flyout and click on the page or pasteboard, or drag to set the table's dimensions. The **Create Table** dialog opens with a selection of preset table formats shown in the **Format** window.

2. Step through the list to preview the layouts and select one. To begin with a plain table, select **Default**.

3. Click **OK**.

The new table appears on the page, and the Table toolbar appears to assist with entering and formatting spreadsheet data.

Manipulating tables

You can select, move, resize, delete, and copy a table and its contents, just as you would with a text frame. Cell properties can also be modified.

To manipulate a table object:

- To resize a table, select it then drag a corner or side handle.

- To move a table, select it and drag an edge when you see the ⊕ cursor.

- To delete a table, select it and press the **Delete** key.

- To duplicate a table and its text, select the table's bounding box, then drag with the **Ctrl** key pressed down.

To select and edit text in cells, rows, and columns:

- To select text in a single cell, double- or triple-click text (for word or paragraph selection) or drag over the text. See Editing text on a page on p. 92.

- To move to the next or previous cells, use the **Tab** or **Shift+Tab** keys, respectively, or the keyboard arrow keys.

- To enter text, simply type into a cell at the insertion point. Cells expand vertically as you type to accommodate extra lines of text. To enter a Tab character, press **Ctrl+Tab**.

- To select a row or column, click its header along the left or top of the table. To select more than one row or column, drag across their headers.

- To select all text (all rows and columns), choose **Select>All** from the Table menu.

- To copy, paste, and delete selected table text within the same table (or between different tables), use the **Copy**, **Paste** and **Delete** commands as you would for frame text. You can also right-click on a cell containing text and choose **Text Menu>Copy**—select a new cell then pick **Paste** from the Edit menu.

- **Fill Right** or **Fill Down** will respectively replicate the contents of a row or column's first cell across the entire selected row or column. Click the row or column header's ▼ button, and choose the option from the flyout menu. To create a sequence of numbers or entries across cells, see Using QuickFill and QuickClear (p. 128).

   The copy and paste of Microsoft Excel spreadsheet cell contents into any PagePlus table is also possible.

- To move cell contents within the same table, select the cell(s), and hover over the cell border(s) until the move cursor is shown—click and drag the cell to its new cell location.

- To format selected text, apply character and paragraph properties or text styles as with any text, from the Text context toolbar (or Format menu).

- To rotate selected text, right-click and choose **Table>Cell Properties**. On the **Orientation** tab, use the rotation dial to set a rotation angle or enter a specific value into the input box.

- Table text can be sorted by row, column, multi-row, multi-column regions or entire table using the **Sort** button from the context toolbar.

- Characters as part of table text can take line, gradient, and bitmap fill properties.

- Table text shares default properties with frame text. For details, see Updating and saving defaults on p. 24.

- 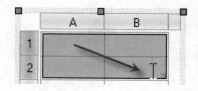 To format numbers and insert formulas, switch on the **Spreadsheet functions** button on the Table context toolbar. For more details, see online Help.

To change the table's structure and appearance:

- To select a cell, click on the edge of the chosen cell. To select more than one cell, click in one cell and drag across the others, one row or column at a time.

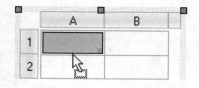

- To **adjust row** or **column size**, drag the cursor shown when hovering over the separating lines in the table row or column headings. Note that you can adjust a row's height independent of the amount of text it contains. For absolute row/column sizing, choose **Set column width(s)** or **Set row height(s)** from the Table menu (or use the right-click menu). For individual columns, click the column or row header's ▼ button, choosing **Set width** or **Set height**. You can resize your columns without affecting the overall table width by adjusting the column heading with **Ctrl**-drag.

- To **distribute** rows or columns, select the entire table or just a selection of rows or columns, then choose **Evenly Distribute>Rows** or **Evenly Distribute>Columns** from the Table menu (or use the right-click menu). To honour table width, a cell's text may wrap when distributing columns.

To evenly distribute rows in a column, click the column's ▼ button and choose **Evenly Distribute Rows**. Conversely, use the equivalent button (and **Evenly Distribute Columns** command) at a row header to distribute columns on the chosen row.

- Choose **Autofit to Contents>Column(s)** from the Table menu (or right-click menu) to reduce or increase the size of selected columns to fit to the text of the greatest width. An equivalent option exists for rows.

  For an individual column or row, click its header's ▼ button, choosing **Autofit Row to Contents** or **Autofit Column to Contents**, respectively.

- To delete multiple rows or columns, select them (or cell text), then choose **Delete** from the Table menu (**Table>Delete** from the right-click menu), then either **Row(s)** or **Column(s)** from the submenu. For an individual column or row, click the header's ▼ button and choose **Delete**.

- To **insert/remove** columns in an existing table, click and drag left/right on the header after the end of the last table column; columns are added or removed as you drag. For insertion of rows, drag up/down on the header at the end of the last row.

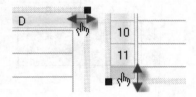

Alternatively, select one or more cells, then choose **Insert** from the Table menu (**Table>Insert** from the right-click menu), then either **Rows...** or **Columns...** from the submenu. In the dialog, specify how many to add, and whether to add them before or after the selected cells.

- To merge cells into larger cells that span more than one row or column (for example, a column head), select a range of cells and choose **Merge Cells** from the Table menu (**Table>Merge Cells** from the right-click menu). The merged cell displays only the text originally visible in the top left selected cell. The original cells and their text are preserved, however—to restore them, select the merged cell and choose **Separate Cells** from the Table menu (**Table>Separate Cells** from the right-click menu).

  To merge all cells in an individual column or row, click the column or row header's ▼ button, choosing **Merge Cells**. Do the equivalent with the **Separate Cells** command to split cells.

- To **copy** cell contents (including text, formatting, borders, and colours) to a new cell in the same table, select the cell(s), press the **Ctrl** key and hover over the cell border(s) until the copy cursor is shown—click and drag the copied cell to its new cell location. Alternatively, select the cell(s), **Copy** and then **Paste** (both via the Edit menu) into a new cell while holding down the **Shift** key.

- To apply a coloured background to a whole table, hover over the top-left hand corner of the table until you see a cursor—click once, and then use the Colour tab or Swatches tab to apply a colour fill. (See Applying solid fills on p. 189).

- To apply a coloured background to specific cells, select the cell(s) and again use the Colour tab or Swatches tab to colour the cells.

Using AutoFormat

To use style presets to customize the table's appearance:

- Choose **AutoFormat...** from the Table menu. The dialog presents a list of sample tables, which differ in their use of **Lines** (inner and outer cell borders), **Fill** (cell and table), **Font** (bold, italic, etc.), and **Alignment** (left, centre, etc.).

- You can pick any sample and use the check boxes to specify which of the sample's attribute(s) to apply to your actual table. This lets you "mix and match," for example by applying (in two passes) the Colour from one sample and the Font from another.

- To restore plain formatting, choose **[Default]**.

Setting Cell Properties

To customize the appearance of one or more cells "by hand":

1. Select the cell(s), row(s) or column(s).

2. Click the ▦ **Cell Properties** button on the Table context toolbar.
   OR

   For a whole column or row only, click the column or row header's ▼ button, choosing **Cell Properties...**.

3. Use the dialog's **Border**, **Fill**, **Transparency**, **Margins**, and **Orientation** tabs to apply cell formatting, then click **OK**.

Using QuickClear and QuickFill

QuickClear and **QuickFill** are handy shortcuts built into tables. Both employ the small "QuickFill handle" which you may have noticed at the lower right of each selected cell (or range of cells).

QuickClear lets you instantly clear a range of cells whereas **QuickFill** lets you quickly enter a standard sequence of numbers or entries, e.g. a number, letter, a month of the year, day of the week, or any arithmetic progression. You can also use QuickFill to replicate one cell's contents over a range of cells.

To QuickClear a range of cells:

1. Select the range to be cleared.

2. Drag the QuickFill handle upward until no cells are specified.

To QuickFill a sequence of entries:

1. Type the first entry of the sequence into the starting cell.

2. Drag the selected cell's QuickFill handle out to the range of cells to be quickfilled, as shown below. The function works both backwards and forwards!

If there are not enough items in the QuickFill sequence, the entries wrap back to the beginning value in the sequence.

To replicate a cell's contents over a range of cells:

1. Click to select the cell whose contents you want to replicate.

2. Drag out the cell's QuickFill handle over the range you want to fill.

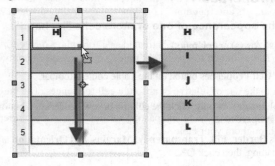

In the example, an alphabetic sequence has been created down a series of cells beginning with the letter "H."

For **numerical sequences**, if the starting selection contains two or more cells, QuickFill uses the difference between them as the common difference. For example, if the first two cells contain the numbers 10 and 20, then the 'quickfilled' sequence would be: 10, 20, 30, ... If only a single number is specified, then the common difference between the numbers will be 1.

Similarly, for **non-numerical sequences**, you can specify a step between any entries, for example, enter "January" in the first cell, "March" in the second. QuickFill will place every other month in the sequence: "January, March, May, July, ..."

You can type also phrases including **known sequences**, and QuickFill will fill the sequence, along with the other words. For example, type "Week 1" and QuickFill would give you the sequence "Week 1, Week 2, Week 3, ..." or "Jan Sales" would give: "Jan Sales, Feb Sales, Mar Sales, ..."

Formatting numbers

The Table toolbar includes additional buttons, switched on with the **Spreadsheet functions** button, that let you vary how numbers are displayed. Number formats let you add commas and currency signs to numbers, express numbers as percents, control how many decimal places are displayed, etc. Number formats *do not* alter numbers internally—only the way numbers are displayed.

See PagePlus help for more information.

Inserting formulas

A table cell can display the result of a **formula** combining values of other cells with arithmetic operators and functions. Formulas are recalculated whenever values in the table change, so they're always up to date.

Any cell starting with the character "=" is treated as a formula. To enter or edit formulas, use the Table context toolbar's edit field. Note that you can only select or edit an entire formula, not just part of it.

PagePlus lets you make use of relative or absolute cell references. The latter makes use of the $ symbol before a column and/or row reference (A1, $A1, A$1) and can be used when copying and pasting formulas, in order to reference a constant value throughout your table.

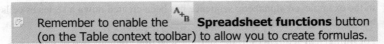

Remember to enable the $^{A}_{+B}$ **Spreadsheet functions** button (on the Table context toolbar) to allow you to create formulas.

To display a cell's formula for editing in the Table context toolbar's edit field:

- Click to select the cell containing the formula.

To enter a formula:

- Click the f_x ▾ **Function** button on the Table context toolbar and choose a specific function from the drop-down menu.
  For example, if you start with a blank cell and choose **SUM()**, PagePlus adds "=SUM()" to the edit field and positions the text cursor between the brackets so that you can type numbers or cell references straight away.
  OR

- Click the **Function** button once to insert an equal sign (=) into the edit field (or type "=" yourself), then continue to type the formula.

Click the ✓ **Accept** button to update the selected cell or click ✕ **Cancel**.

See the PagePlus Help for a more detailed explanation of operators, percentages, values and functions used in formulas.

Inserting a calendar

The **Calendar Wizard** helps you design month-at-a-glance calendars for use in your publication.

The calendar is created as a scalable text-based table so you can edit text using the standard text tools. The properties of a selected calendar are similar to those of a table, and can be modified identically (see Manipulating tables on p. 123).

The wizard lets you set up the month/year and calendar style/format, and controls the inclusion of personal events and/or public holidays. The **Calendar Event Manager** lets you add personal events before or after adding a calendar to the page. The **Calendar Event Manager** lets you add personal events before or after adding a calendar to the page.

If you have adopted a calendar-based design template, you'll be initially prompted to configure **global** calendar details via a User Details dialog. This updates all calendar details throughout your PagePlus document—in the same way that you'd set up the date (along with the time) on some alarm clocks.

For calendar-specific properties, a context toolbar lets you change an existing calendar's month/year, modify calendar-specific properties, and manage calendar events (both personal and public holidays).

At any time, you can update calendar details throughout your project via Set User Details—in the same way that you'd set up the date (along with the time) on some alarm clocks. This is especially useful if you want to update the year on a year-to-view Web page, composed of 12 monthly calendars—you only need to change the year in one place.

To insert a calendar:

1. Click the Table flyout on the Tools toolbar and choose **31** **Insert Calendar**.

2. Click again on your page, or drag out to set the desired size of the calendar.

3. From the displayed **Calendar Wizard**, define options for your calendar including setting the year and month, calendar style (square, or in single or double column format), week start day, room to write, display options, switching on personal events/holidays, and calendar format.

4. Click **Finish** to complete the wizard.

To set up your calendar (using calendar design template):

1. Open a calendar design template from the Startup Wizard's **Use Design Template** option.

2. In the displayed **User Details** dialog, select the **Year** that your calendar will adopt from the drop-down menu.

3. In the Events section, check **Show public holidays** and/or **Show personal events** if your template's calendar is to adopt the holidays and events already configured in the Calendar Event Manager (to modify personal events, click the **Events** button).

4. Click the **Update** button.

If you plan to use your calendar in subsequent years, simply update the **Year** setting in **Tools>Set User Details** (use the dialog's Calendars tab if not shown).

To view and edit a selected calendar's properties:

1. Click the **Edit Calendar** button on the Calendar context toolbar.

2. Choose an appropriate tab and make your modification, then press **OK**.

Right-click (with the **Calendar** option selected) also lets you select, insert, distribute, delete, and adjust widths/heights for rows (or columns), as well as autofit to cell contents, but take care not to corrupt your table formatting!

Adding public holidays

When you create a calendar you can set up the appropriate public holidays for the country you reside in. The holidays will show up in your calendar automatically if **Add public holidays** is checked in Calendar Properties.

To enable public holidays:

1. Select your calendar's bounding box, and click **Edit Calendar** button on the context toolbar.

2. From the Events tab, check **Add public holidays**.

3. (Optional) Swap to a different country's public holiday settings by using the **Region** drop-down list.

4. Click **OK**.

To add public holidays:

1. Select your calendar's bounding box.

2. Click **Calendar Events** on the context toolbar.

3. Enable the **Show public holidays** option.

4. Click the **Save** button.

Adding personal events

You can complement your public holiday listings (e.g., Easter holidays) by adding personal events such as birthdays, anniversaries, and bill payments (unfortunately!) so that the events show up on your calendar—simply use the **Calendar Events** button on a selected calendar's context toolbar. Events show automatically on your calendar under the chosen date.

To enable personal events:

1. Select your calendar's bounding box, and click **Edit Calendar** button on the context toolbar.

2. From the Events tab, check **Add personal events**.

3. Click **OK**.

To add an event:

1. Select your calendar's bounding box.

2. Click **Calendar Events** on the context toolbar.

3. Ensure that the **Show personal events** option is selected.

4. (Optional) Select **Show events by date** to view your events in a more traditional calendar layout.

5. Click the ▤ **New event** button.

6. From the dialog, type, use the up/down arrows, or click the ⬚ **Browse** button to select a date.

7. Enter your event text into the text input box. This displays in your calendar under the chosen date.

8. If the event is a birthday or other annual event, check **Event recurs annually**.

9. Click **OK**. The event appears in the event list under the chosen date.

10. When you have finished adding events, click **Save**.

Use the ▤ **Edit event** or ✕ **Delete event** buttons to modify or delete an existing event.

Inserting database tables

As a great way of producing a database report in your publication, it is possible for a database table to be imported and presented as a PagePlus table. The database table could be from one of a comprehensive range of database file formats (Serif databases (*.sdb), Microsoft Access, dBASE), as well as from HTML files, Excel files, ODBC, and various delimited text files.

For multi-table databases, PagePlus lets you select the table to be inserted.

For a high degree of control, it is also possible to filter and sort your database records prior to import.

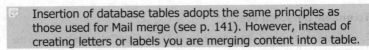

> Insertion of database tables adopts the same principles as those used for Mail merge (see p. 141). However, instead of creating letters or labels you are merging content into a table.

To insert a database table:

1. Click 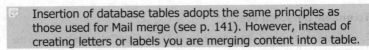 **Insert Database table** from the Tools toolbar's Table flyout.

2. Using the pointer, draw an area on your page that will contain your database information.

> If there are many fields in your database table you may consider presenting the information on a page with landscape orientation. Alternatively, you can choose only a subset of those fields (see below).

3. In the dialog, navigate to your database file and select it. Use the drop-down menu to change file format if you can't find the database file you require.

4. Click **Open**.

5. (Optional; for multi-table databases) The **Select Table** dialog displays the tables within your database. Select your table and click **OK**.

6. The **Merge List** dialog shows all the table rows (records) in the table—choose to **Select All** records, **Toggle Select** (invert all current selections) or use a custom **Filter...** The filter option also lets you sort the records to be merged. The **Edit...** button lets you edit Serif Database SDB files only. Click **OK**.

7. The list of fields available in the table is shown in the **Select Fields** dialog. Uncheck any fields that you don't want to be included in the import process. Again, Select All, Select None, or Toggle Select options are available.

8. Click the **OK** button. The database table appears on your page.

Filtering your records

Records can be filtered via the Merge List's **Filter...** button by using the Filter Records tab then subsequently sorted into any combination with the accompanying Sort Records tab. The option helps you limit the number of records imported to only those you require.

Note that the Boolean operator "And" and "Or" operator to build up your filter criteria row-by-row.

The Sort Records tab is used to sort by three prioritized field names, either in ascending or descending order.

Creating a table of contents

The Table of Contents Wizard (**Insert>Table of Contents...**) helps you create a table of contents with up to six levels of headings and sub-headings derived from named styles in your publication. PagePlus includes built-in text styles intended specifically for table of contents preparation: "Contents-Title" and "Contents-1st" through "Contents-6th". Using the Wizard, you'll specify which named styles should map to the three Contents styles. For example, you could pull out all text using the "Heading" style as your first-level headings. You can update the Contents styles as needed (see Using text styles on p. 104).

If you're exporting to PDF format, PagePlus can automatically build a bookmark list using the same style markings in your text.

To create a table of contents:

1. Decide which named styles you want to designate as headings at each of up to six levels.

2. Check your publication to make sure these styles are used consistently.

3. Review the choices you'll need to make when you run the Table of Contents Wizard.

4. From the Insert menu, choose **Table of Contents...** to run the Wizard.

5. You can easily modify the look of your table of contents, or run the Wizard again to update the information.

Using styles to prepare a table of contents

The Wizard will show you a list of all the style names used in your publication, and you will check boxes to include text of a given style as a heading at a particular level (1 through 6). For example, you could pull out all text using the "Heading" style as your first-level headings.

Entries in the resulting table of contents will appear in the order the text occurs in your publication.

When the table of contents is created, PagePlus formats it using built-in text styles intended specifically for table of contents preparation: "Contents-Title" and "Contents-1st" through "Contents-6th". You can easily change the look of your table of contents by changing the style definitions for these built-in "Contents" styles.

Creating an index

An **index** is a valuable reader aid in a longer document such as a report or manual. The Index Wizard helps you create an index with **main entries** and **subentries**, based on **index entry marks** you insert in frame, table, or artistic text.

To mark index entries:

1. Select a portion of text or click for an insertion point before the first word you want to mark and then choose **Edit Story** from the Edit menu. The WritePlus window opens.

2. Click the ⬚ **Mark Index** button on the Story toolbar.

3. Use the **Mark Index Entry** dialog to edit index entry marks in the Main entry or Subentry box.

   If you selected a word or phrase in the story, it appears as the Main entry in the dialog. You can use the entry as it is, or type new text for the main entry and Sub-entry (if any). You must include a main entry for each sub-entry. The dialog's scrolling list records entries and sub-entries alphabetically.

   > Index entry marks are invisible on the PagePlus screen and can only be added or edited in WritePlus.

   - To reuse an index entry, click it in the scrolling list.

   - For a standard index entry, leave the **Current page** box enabled.

   - To insert a cross-reference with the term(s) preceded by "See:", enable **Cross-reference** (to include a word other than "See," simply replace it in the box).

     - You can also specify a bold and/or italic page number format.

4. Click **Mark** to insert the new entry mark or update a selected mark.

To build an index:

1. First mark the entries as described above.

2. Choose **Index...** from the Insert menu.

3. Run through the Index Wizard, choosing where to place and how to format your index. Repeat at any time to update the information.

Producing a book with BookPlus

BookPlus is a management utility built into PagePlus that lets you produce a whole book from a set of separate PagePlus (*.PPP) publication files. Using BookPlus, you can arrange the chapter files in a specific order, systematically renumber pages, synchronize styles and other elements between all chapters, create a Table of Contents and/or Index for the whole book, and output the book via printing, PostScript®, or PDF. BookPlus can perform all these managerial tasks whether or not the original files are open! Your settings are saved as a compact BookPlus (*.PPB) book file, separate from the source publication files.

Working with books and chapters

A book consists of a set of PagePlus (*.PPP) publication files. Each publication file is considered a chapter in the book. To create a new book, you'll need at least one constituent chapter file.

To create a new book:

- In PagePlus, on the File menu, choose **New** and then click **New Book...**.

BookPlus opens with an empty dialog reserved for the **chapter list**.

To add a chapter to the chapter list:

1. In BookPlus, on the Chapter menu, click 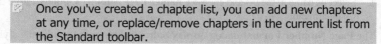 **Add...**
2. In the dialog, select one or more PagePlus files to be added as chapters. (Use the **Ctrl** or **Shift** keys to select multiple files or a range of files.) Click **Open**.

The selected files appear in the chapter list, which can be reordered by dragging.

> Once you've created a chapter list, you can add new chapters at any time, or replace/remove chapters in the current list from the Standard toolbar.

To save the current chapter list as a book file:

- Choose Save (or **Save As...**) from the BookPlus File menu.

> You can open saved book files from PagePlus using **File>Open...**. You can have more than one book file open at a time.

Numbering pages

BookPlus provides a variety of options for incrementing page numbers continuously from one chapter to another, through the whole book. Page numbers will only appear on pages or (more commonly) master pages where you've inserted page number fields. To "suppress" page numbers—for example, on a title page—simply don't include a page number field there.

BookPlus lets you change page number style choices you've made in the original file (using **Format/Page Number Format...** in PagePlus), and provides other options such as inserting a blank page when necessary to force new chapters to start on a right-hand page. You don't need to have the original files open to update page numbering.

To set page numbering options for the book:

1. Choose **Book Page Number Options...** from the BookPlus File menu.

2. In the dialog, select whether you want page numbers to **Continue from previous chapter**, **Continue on next odd page**, or **Continue on next even page**. Typically you'll want new chapters to start on odd (right-hand or "recto") pages.

3. Leave **Insert blank page when necessary** checked if you want to output an extra page at the end of a chapter where the next page number (if you've selected odd- or even-page continuation) would otherwise skip a page. Either way, BookPlus will number your pages correctly—but for correct imposition in professional printing it's usually best to insert the blank page. **Note:** You won't see the blank page inserted into your original file, only in the generated output.

4. Click **OK**. BookPlus immediately applies your settings to all chapters.

To set page numbering options for a chapter:

1. Select its name in the list and choose **Chapter Page Number Options...** from the Chapter menu.

The **Page Number Format** dialog displays current settings for numbering style and initial numbering.

2. To change the numbering style, make a selection in the Style section. For example, you might use lowercase Roman numerals for a preface.

3. To force page numbering to start at a certain value, uncheck **Continue from previous chapter** and type the starting value. For example, you might want to skip page numbering for introductory ("front") matter and begin numbering from "1" on the first page of main body text.

4. Click **OK**. BookPlus immediately applies your settings to the selected chapter. **Note:** These settings only apply to the selected chapter.

If you've reordered chapters or changed the chapter list in any way, you can quickly reimpose correct numbering on the current list.

To update page numbering:

- Choose **Renumber Pages** from the BookPlus File menu.

Synchronizing chapters

Synchronizing means imposing consistent styles, palettes, and/or colour schemes throughout the book. This is accomplished by using one chapter (called the **style source**) as a model for the rest of the book. You define attributes in the style source chapter, and then select which attributes should be adjusted in other chapters to conform to the style source. For example, you could redefine the "Normal" text style in your style source chapter, then quickly propagate that change through the rest of the book. The Modified and Synchronized columns of the BookPlus chapter list let you keep track of recent file changes.

To set one chapter as the style source:

- Select its name in the chapter list and choose **Set Style Source** from the Chapter menu.

The current style source is identified in the Synchronized column of the chapter list.

To synchronize one or more chapters with the style source:

1. To update just certain chapters, make sure their names are selected in the chapter list.

2. Choose **Synchronize...** from the File menu.

3. In the dialog, select whether you want to update **All** or just **Selected** chapters. Check which attributes should be updated to conform to those defined in the style source file: **Text styles**, **Object styles**, **Colour scheme**, and/or **Colour palette**.

4. Click **OK**.

BookPlus imposes the specified changes and updates the Synchronized time in the chapter list for each selected file. If the file was altered in any way, the Modified time updates as well.

Building a Table of Contents or Index

From BookPlus, you can build a **Table of Contents** and/or **Index** that includes entries for the entire set of chapters. In each case, you'll need to begin by designating a specific chapter where the resulting pages should be added.

To create a table of contents or index for the book:

1. In the chapter list, select the name of the chapter file where you want to add the table of contents or index.

2. Choose **Insert** from the Chapter menu and select **Table of Contents...** or **Index...** from the submenu.

BookPlus opens the chapter file if it's not already open, and the Wizard for the procedure you've selected appears.

3. Select **Yes** when the Wizard asks if you want to build a table of contents or index for the entire book. Continue clicking **Next>** and selecting choices in the Wizard.

Printing and PDF output

When you **print** or generate **PDF output** from BookPlus, you'll have the choice of printing the entire book or selected chapters.

To print the book or selected chapters:

1. To print just certain chapters, make sure their names are selected in the chapter list.

2. Choose **Print...** from the BookPlus File menu.

3. Under "Print Range" on the General tab, select **Entire book** to output all chapters, or **Selected chapters** to output just those you selected. You can also select the **Pages** option to output one or more specific page(s). Whichever option you've chosen, a drop-down list lets you export all sheets in the range, or just odd or even sheets.
   Note: If you select **Print to file** to output PostScript, BookPlus will generate a separate file for each chapter.

4. Set other options as detailed in Printing basics on p . 203, then click **Print**.

To export the book or selected chapters as PDF:

1. To export just certain chapters, make sure their names are selected in the chapter list.

2. Choose **Publish as PDF...** from the BookPlus File menu.

3. Under "Print Range" on the General tab, select **Entire book** to output all chapters, or **Selected chapters** to output just those you selected. You can also select the **Pages** option to output one or more specific page(s). Whichever option you've chosen, a drop-down list lets you export all pages in the range, or just odd or even pages.

4. Set other options as detailed in Exporting PDF files on p . 213, then click **OK**.

Using mail merge

Most commonly, **mail merge** means printing your publication a number of times, inserting different information each time from a **data source** such as an address list file—for example into a series of letters or mailing labels.

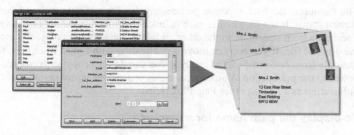

PagePlus can handle many kinds of data sources and more challenging creative tasks. It is even possible to merge picture data (for example, digital photos) into single fields or even auto-create a grid layout of pictures and text suitable for catalogues or photo albums.

As mail merge is an advanced feature of PagePlus, see the PagePlus Help for more detail. Subjects covered include:

- Opening a data source.

- Editing Serif Database files.

- Selecting, filtering, and sorting the merge list.

- Inserting placeholders for your data.

- Previewing data in the publication.

- Merging and printing.

Checking fonts and resources used

The **Resource Manager** lists the fonts and resources used in your publication, and shows if the pictures are linked to external picture files or embedded within the document. In addition, it will allow font substitution after import of PDF or opening of PagePlus files; this is necessary when fonts used in the publications are not available on your PC.

To display the Resource Manager:

- Choose **Resource Manager...** from the Tools menu.

Resources tab

The Resources tab lists imported pictures, media, Java applets, etc. and their current status. It shows whether each is linked or embedded and lets you switch a resource from one mode to the other. "Linked" data consists of a reference to the original file. If you copy or move a publication with linked resources, for example from one computer to another, you should also copy any resource files linked to the publication. You can make this process easier by saving the publication as a package (see PagePlus Help).

To display the path name for a resource:

- Click on the resource name.

- The path appears below the Resources section.

To view a particular item:

- Double-click its name in the list.
  OR
  Select the item's name and click **Display**.

To switch an item from linked to embedded:

1. Select the item's name.

2. Click **Embed** to embed a linked item.

Conversely, click **Make Linked** to link an embedded item.

To check whether pictures you import are to be linked or embedded:

- Choose **Options...** from the Tools menu and click the **General** tab.

- Check **Suggest embed/link picture** for embedding or linking. Set a file size below which files are embedded automatically.

Fonts tab

The Fonts tab lists fonts used in text objects on individual pages or throughout the whole publication, along with their current status. The status column can display "OK" or "Missing". If "Missing" is shown then the font is not available on your PC. For this reason, if you are copying a publication to take to a different computer, you should check that the fonts used are available on the new computer or save the publication as a package (see PagePlus Help).

A third column called Substitutions shows which local fonts are being used as substitutes for missing fonts. See Substituting fonts on p. 100 for more information.

To display the font category:

- Click on the font name.

The font category (TrueType, Printer, or System) appears below the Fonts section.

To view a particular item:

- Double-click its name in the list.
  OR
  Select the item's name and click **Display**.

Images, Lines,
and Shapes

Importing pictures

PagePlus lets you insert pictures from a wide variety of file formats, including bitmaps, vector images, and metafiles, and in several different ways. Here's a quick overview:

- **Bitmapped pictures**, also known as **bitmaps** or **raster pictures**, are built from a matrix of dots ("pixels"), rather like the squares on a sheet of graph paper. They may originate as digital camera photos or scanned pictures, or be created (or enhanced) with a "paint" program or photo editor. Typical examples include GIF, JPG, PNG, and the new HD Photo (WDP).

- **Draw** graphics, also known as **vector images**, are resolution-independent and contain drawing commands such as "draw a line from A to B."

- **Metafiles** are the native graphics format for Windows and combine raster and vector information. Serif also has its own metafile format, **Serif MetaFile Format (SMF)** , which is optimized for image sharing between Serif applications.

You can also acquire pictures directly from PhotoCDs or via TWAIN devices (scanners or digital cameras)—see PagePlus help.

Inserting pictures

There are several ways to bring a picture into PagePlus. You can drag a file from an external Windows folder directly onto your page, drag a thumbnail from PagePlus's Media bar, or import a picture as an embedded or linked image via a dialog... even place it into a picture frame.

- **Detached** pictures float freely on a page, while **inline** images are incorporated with the text flow in a text object.

- **Embedded** pictures become part of the publication file, while **linking** places a reference copy of the picture on the page and preserves a connection to the original file. Each approach has its pros and cons (see Embedding vs. Linking on p. 149).

- ⊠ **Picture frames** let you add your picture into a previously applied shaped frame. Choose from elliptical, star, heart, and triangular frames, amongst many others.

To import a picture from a file:

1. To place the picture:
   - inline with the text - click for an insertion point in a text object.
   - detached from the text - make sure all text objects are deselected.
   - into a frame - create the frame and then select it (see above).

2. *In the main window:*

   Click the ⬛ **Import Picture...** button on the Tools toolbar's Picture flyout.

   In WritePlus:

   Choose **Picture File...** from the **Insert** menu.

3. Use the dialog to select the picture to open.

4. Select either **Embed picture** or **Link picture** to include or exclude the picture from the project, respectively. Use linked pictures to minimize project file size.

5. If you select the **Place at native dpi** option and the picture has a different internal setting, PagePlus will scale it accordingly; otherwise it applies a screen resolution setting of **96 dpi**. Either way—or if you resize it downwards later on—the picture retains all its original picture data until it's published. Check Place as raster if you want to permanently convert an imported EPS, Windows Metafile or Serif Metafile to a bitmap.

6. Click **Open**.

7. If there's a text insertion point in the main window, you'll be prompted whether to insert the picture at the current cursor position. Click **Yes** if you want to do this.

   ⬛ The mouse pointer changes to the **Picture Paste** cursor if there was no insertion point (or you answered **No** to the prompt). What you do next determines the initial size and placement of the detached picture.

8. To insert the picture at a default size, simply click the mouse.
   OR
   To set the size of the inserted picture, drag out a region and release the mouse button.

To replace a picture:

- Click the ⬛ button shown under the selected frame.

Embedding vs. linking

Embedding means the picture in PagePlus is now distinct from the original file. Embedding results in a larger PagePlus file, and if you need to alter an embedded picture you'll need to re-import it after editing. Still, it's the best choice if file size isn't an issue and graphics are final.

Linking inserts a copy of the picture file into the PagePlus publication, linked to the actual file so that any changes you later make to it in the native application will be automatically reflected in PagePlus. Linking is one way of avoiding "bloat" by limiting the size of the publication file. On the other hand, you'll need to manage the externally linked files carefully, for example making sure to include them all if you move the PagePlus file to a different drive.

By default, PagePlus prompts you to embed pictures that are smaller than 256 KB, by preselecting the "Embed Picture" option in the Insert Picture dialog (but you can always select "Link Picture" instead). If you like, you can change the threshold file size or even switch off the automatic selection.

You can use the Resource Manager later on, to change an item's status from linked to embedded, or vice versa.

For dragging images from the Media Bar, images <256 KB are embedded, while images >256 KB are linked. However, you can change embed or link status with the **Shift** key as you drag.

To preselect embedding or linking based on file size:

1. Choose **Options...** from the Tools menu. You'll see the **General** tab.

2. To preselect the "Embed Picture" option for pictures under a certain size, select the threshold size in the "Embed if smaller than" list. ("Link Picture" will be pre-selected for pictures larger than the threshold.)

3. To choose whether to embed or link each picture, uncheck **Suggest embed/link picture**. You can still select either option in the import dialog; it will now remember and preselect the last setting you used.

Adding picture frames

Not to be confused with a decorative border, a **picture frame** is a shaped
container similar to a text frame. You can select any one of a series of shaped
empty frames as a placeholder, and then import or drag a picture into it. At any
time you can swap a different picture into the same frame. This gives you the
flexibility of separating the container from its content—you can incorporate the
picture frame into your layout irrespective of the actual picture that will go
inside it.

You may encounter picture frames if you use photo-rich design templates such
as those found in the Photo Album template category. When loaded, the picture
frames display as blank placeholders ready for adding your own pictures (from
the Media Bar or by using Replace Picture).

All picture frames, when selected, display a supporting Picture frame toolbar
under the frame which offers panning, rotation (90 degrees anti-clockwise),
zoom in, zoom out, and replace picture options (shown below from left to right).

Picture frames are always detached, i.e. they float freely on the page.

To add a picture to a frame:

1. For an empty square frame, choose **Picture>Empty Frame...** from the **Insert**
    menu.
    OR
    For a frame of a particular shape, e.g. **Elliptical Picture Frame**, choose a shape
    on the Import Picture flyout on the Tools toolbar.

2. The mouse pointer changes to the **Picture Paste** cursor. What you do next
    determines the initial size and placement of the picture frame.

3. To insert the frame at a default size, simply click the mouse.
   OR
   To set the size of the frame, drag out a region and release the mouse button.

4. From the Media Bar's currently displayed album, drag and drop a photo directly onto the picture frame.

> Take advantage of the Gallery tab to drag and drop various bordered and basic picture frames onto your page. Choose from frames of different orientations and styles.

The picture is added to the frame using default Picture Frame properties, i.e. it is scaled to maximum fit. However, you can alter the picture's size, orientation and positioning relative to its frame; aspect ratio is always maintained.

To change picture size and positioning:

Select a populated picture frame, and from the accompanying Picture Frame toolbar:

- Click the button to position the photo in the picture frame by panning.

- Click the button to rotate the photo in 90 degree anti-clockwise increments.

- Click the button to zoom in/out of the photo.

OR

1. Right-click on a picture frame and choose **Properties>Frame Properties...**.
   OR
   Select the picture frame and choose **Frame Properties** on the Picture context toolbar.

2. In the dialog, you can scale to maximum/minimum, **Stretch to Fit**, or use the original image's size (**No Scale**).

3. To change vertical alignment of pictures within the frames, select **Top**, **Middle**, or **Bottom**.

4. For horizontal alignment, select **Left**, **Centre**, or **Right**.

While you can take advantage of PagePlus's preset frames you can create your own shape (e.g., a morphed QuickShape or closed curve) then convert it to a picture frame.

Creating custom picture frames

1. Create the shape as required.

2. Right-click the shape and select **Convert to Picture Frame**.
   OR
   Select **Convert to>Picture Frame** from the Tools menu.

You can then add a picture to the frame as described previously.

Using the Media Bar

The Media Bar acts as a "basket" containing photos for inclusion in your publication. Its chief use is to aid the design process by improving efficiency (avoiding having to import photos one by one) and convenience (making photos always-at-hand). For photo-rich documents in particular, perhaps based on Photo Album design templates, the Media Bar is a valuable tool for dragging photos directly into picture frames or for simply replacing existing pictures on the page.

You can even use the **AutoFlow** feature to add all photos sequentially into available empty picture frames with one click.

The bar can be used as a temporary storage area before placing photos in your document, or it can be used to create more permanent photo albums from which you can retrieve stored photos at any time. By default, photos are added to a **temporary album** but remember to click the New Album button if you want to save your album for later use. Each time you start PagePlus you simply load that saved album (or any other saved album) or just work with a temporary album—the choice is yours!

Photo albums can be subsequently modified, renamed and deleted—viewing the contents of an individual album or all albums at the same time is possible.

You can import an unlimited number of photos by file or by whole folders, and set photo resolution (native or 96dpi) and whether photos are embedded or linked to your project in advance of photo placement on the page.

For large photo collections, searching throughout albums for photos by file name and EXIF, IPTC or XMP metadata is possible in the search box at the top of the Media Bar; even edit XMP metadata from within PagePlus.

> The currently loaded album shown on your Media Bar will remain visible irrespective of which document you have open.

Photo thumbnails can be dragged from the Media Bar directly onto your page, into an existing standalone photo, or into an empty or populated picture frame.

To view the Media Bar:

- Unless already displayed, click the ▬▬ handle at the bottom of your workspace.

To add photos to a temporary album:

1. With the Media Bar visible and a temporary album loaded, click on the Media Bar's workspace to reveal an **Open** dialog.

2. From the dialog, navigate to a photo or folder, select photo(s), and optionally choose whether your photos are to be placed at native or 96 dpi, or embedded or linked (embedding may increase your file size significantly).

3. Click **Open**. Your photos appear as thumbnails in the Menu Bar workspace.

> Unless you save it, the temporary album and its photo contents will not be saved when you close PagePlus.

> You can drag one or more files from any Windows folder directly into the Media Bar window. If you right-click an image in the Media Bar and choose Locate in Explorer you'll open the photo's folder via Windows Explorer—great for drag and drop or just general file management!

To save a temporary album to a named album:

1. Click the down arrow on the **Add To** button. From the menu, select **New Album**.

2. In the **New Album** dialog, in the **Album Name** box, type a name to identify your album in the future.

3. (Optional) For any photo you can alter the resolution (native or 96 dpi), or embed/link status in advance of placement on your page—click a photo's setting and use the setting's drop-down menu to change. You can also change these settings during drag/drop onto the page.

4. Click **OK**.

To include a temporary album's photos in an existing saved album, click the **Add To** button and choose a named album from the menu.

To create a named album:

1. Click the bar's **New Album** button.

2. In the dialog, in the **Album Name** box, type a name to identify your album in the future.

3. Click the **Add Image...** or **Add Folder...** button.

4. In the dialog, navigate to a photo or folder and optionally choose whether your photos are to be placed at native or 96 dpi, or embedded or linked (embedding increases your file size significantly). Click **Open**.

5. The **New Album** dialog lists the files for inclusion. Optionally, alter DPI and Embed options by clicking on each photo's setting, then selecting from the drop-down menu.

6. Click **OK**.

To load a saved album:

- Select a saved album name from the bar's top-right drop-down menu. The album's photos will display in the workspace.

Manage A saved album can be selected as above and then modified via the **Manage** button (only shown for existing saved albums). You can add photos/folders, delete photos, change DPI, and alter embed/link status.

To rename or delete an album:

- Right-click an existing album name in the top-right drop-down menu and choose **Rename Album...** or **Delete Album...**.

To sort results from an album:

- In the **Sort By** search box, enter your search criteria. Any matching files will be displayed in the bar's workspace.

Adding photos to the page

To add a photo to your page:

1. Display the Media Bar's temporary album or load a saved album from the top-right drop-down menu.

2. Drag an album's photo thumbnail onto the page—either as a detached photo, or directly into a picture frame.
   OR
   Use the **AutoFlow** feature.

AutoFlow—adding content automatically

AutoFlow lets you flow the photos currently displayed in the Media Bar throughout empty picture **frames** spread throughout your publication (you can't reflow photos once frames are populated with content). This is especially useful when using Photo Album design templates or other photo-rich documents.

To use this feature, you must have multiple picture frames present in your current document, as well as a range of photos present in your Media Bar. The autoflow process involves a simple click of the mouse button.

To automatically flow your photos:

- Click the [AutoFlow] button to the right of the bar's workspace. The photos are placed sequentially in your document's available picture frames in the order they appear in the Media Bar.

A dialog will display if you've more picture frames than you have photos and vice versa. To resolve, either remove extra pages or add more frames then add any remaining photos by drag and drop. A placed photo's thumbnail shows a green check in its bottom-right corner, while a photo that is not yet placed will not show the check.

Using the Gallery

The **Gallery** tab serves as a container for storing your own design objects you'd like to reuse in different publications. It also includes sample designs and is stocked with a wide variety of pre-designed elements that you can customize and use as a starting point for your own designs. Once you've copied a design to the Gallery, it becomes available in any publication—simply open the Gallery!

To view the Gallery tab:

- The **Gallery** tab is by default docked with other tabs. If not displayed, go to **View>Studio Tabs** and select the **Gallery** tab.

The Gallery has two parts: (1) an upper **Categories** drop-down menu and (2) a lower **Designs** window showing a list of thumbnails representing the designs in the selected category. You can adopt a design by dragging the thumbnail onto the page.

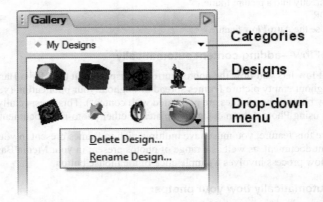

The Gallery tab also lets you store your own designs under My Designs (or in a user-defined category) if you would like to reuse them—the design is made available in any PagePlus project. When you first install PagePlus, the My Designs gallery will be empty. You can add and delete any items stored in My Designs or one of its categories, with the option of naming elements to facilitate rapid retrieval by searching.

> Designs cannot be added to/removed from any pre-defined category.

To use a design from the Gallery:

- Click its thumbnail in the design category and drag it out onto the page. The Gallery retains a copy of the design until you expressly delete it.

To view your Gallery:

1. Click the Studio's **Gallery** tab.

2. Select a folder or category from the drop-down menu. The items from the folder's first listed category are displayed by default.

To add, delete, or rename My Design categories:

1. With the Gallery tab selected, click the ▷ **Tab Menu** button and choose **Add category**, **Remove category**, or **Rename category** from the drop-down list.

2. Use the dialog to enter and/or confirm your change.

If adding a category, you need to name the category in a dialog. For removal or deletion, simply pick the category in advance of picking the option.

> All designs in a deleted category will also be lost!

To move or copy an object into the Gallery:

1. Select My Designs or a gallery category within that group into which you want to add the object. Use the Categories drop-down menu for this.

2. To move, drag the object from the page and drop it onto the Designs group in the right category. To copy, press the **Ctrl** key before starting to drag.

3. If the **Prompt to Rename** option is turned on, you'll be prompted to type a name for the design. (You can name or rename the design later, if you wish.) By default, unnamed designs are labelled as "Unnamed."

4. A thumbnail of the design appears in the Designs group, and its name or label appears as a tooltip (Tiny Swatches view) when you hover the pointer over the design, or as a label underneath the icon (all other Swatch views).

To delete a design from the Gallery:

- Click on the drop-down button in the bottom-right corner of a thumbnail (shown by hover over) and choose **Delete Design...** from the menu.

Importing TWAIN images

If your scanner or digital camera provides **TWAIN** support, you can import pictures directly into PagePlus using the TWAIN standard. Or, save the scanned image separately and then import into PagePlus.

To set up your TWAIN device for importing:

- See the documentation supplied with your scanner for operating instructions.

To import a scanned image:

- Choose **Picture...** from the Insert menu, then select **TWAIN** and **Acquire** from the submenu to open a file selection dialog.

If you have more than one TWAIN-compatible device installed, you may need to select which source you wish to scan with.

To select a different TWAIN source for scanning:

1. Choose **Picture...** from the Insert menu, then select **TWAIN** and **Select Source** from the submenu.

2. Identify the device you want to use as your TWAIN source.

Suggestions for image scanning

First the tips... then the theory!

- As a general rule, the optimal scanning resolution for **print work** (in dpi) is about *one-third the dots-per-inch setting* (i.e. twice the resultant lines per inch) on the printer or other device that will be used. If you're printing at 600dpi, then 200 dpi scanning is fine.

- For an image that will end up on a **Web page**, it's possible to get great results scanning at 100dpi, using exactly the screen dimensions you need. If you're going to edit the image, increase the dpi to be on the safe side.

- For **line art** and **halftone images**, save as a black-and-white TIFF, PCX, or GIF.

- For greyscale **photographic images**, scan using greyscales and save as a greyscale TIFF file. If you have a colour scanner, save a colour TIFF. You can resize these images and still maintain reasonable quality, provided you don't make them significantly larger than the original. In general, the number of greyscales or colours is a more important issue than the actual resolution (dpi).

Scanned images, especially colour, can get very large and you need to take this into consideration. Large files take a long time to load, save and print and eat your disk space! One myth is that the higher the resolution of your scanner, the better results you'll achieve. While that's true in theory, the real limit to quality is how the image will ultimately be reproduced. Will it end up on the printed page or on-screen? Either way, the real issue is how many "extra pixels" you'll need in the original scan.

Printed output: If the image will be professionally printed, will that be onto a sheet of newsprint or a glossy coated stock? Paper itself puts a ceiling on reproduction quality. Lower-grade paper tends to spread ink around more easily, so the dots of ink used to print a picture need to be larger. This means a wider halftone screen with fewer lines per inch (lpi).

If you'll generate your output on a desktop printer, the device will be putting bits of toner or droplets of ink on the paper. On a laser printer, shades of grey result from variations in toner coverage. Desktop colour printers create colour by laying down dots of cyan, magenta, yellow, and black ink. Again, printer resolution and paper type are quite variable. **Dpi (dots per inch)** is the most common measure of print quality. But the **lines per inch**, based on halftone reproduction, is equally useful. A print resolution of 600 dpi corresponds to about 100 lpi—that's how we arrived at the 200 dpi scanning recommendation above.

Screen output: If your image will end up on-screen instead of in print, it will no doubt be viewed at standard screen resolution of 96 dpi. (That's why this is the default resolution in PagePlus.) If you're producing Web images, it makes more sense to regard resolution as a fixed factor, and think in terms of image dimensions instead. This means that, for an image that will end up on a Web page without any editing, you can get away with scanning at 100dpi, using the screen dimensions you'll need on the Web page. But that's cutting it close, especially if you'll be editing the image at all.

Using the Image Cutout Studio

Image Cutout Studio offers a powerful integrated solution for cutting objects out from their backgrounds. Depending on the make up of your images you can separate subject of interests from their backgrounds, either by retaining the subject of interest (usually people, objects, etc.) or removing a simple uniform background (e.g., sky, studio backdrop). In both instances, the resulting "cutout" image creates an eye-catching look for your publication.

The latter background removal method is illustrated in the following multi-image example.

The white initial background is discarded, leaving interim checkerboard transparency, from which another image can be used as a more attractive background. A red tint on the second image's background is used to indicate areas to be discarded.

To launch Image Cutout Studio:

1. Select an image to be cut out.

2. Select **Image Cutout Studio** from the displayed Picture context toolbar. Image Cutout Studio is launched.

Choosing an output

It's essential that you choose an output type prior to selecting areas for keeping/discarding. Either an alpha-edged or vector-cropped bitmap can be chosen as your output type prior to selection. The choice you make really depends on the image, in particular how well defined image edges are. Let's look at the output types and explain the difference between each.

Output Type	Description and use
Alpha-edged Bitmap	Use when cutting out objects with poorly defined edges. Transparency and pixel blending are used at the outline edge to produce professional results with negligible interference from background colours. The term "alpha" refers to a 32-bit image's alpha transparency channel.
Vector-cropped Bitmap	Use on more well-defined edges. A cropped image with crop outline is created which can be later manipulated with the crop tools. You can optionally apply feathering to the image edge but will not remove background colour.

To create an alpha-edged bitmap:

1. Select **Alpha-edged Bitmap** from the **Output Type** drop-down menu.

2. (Optional) Drag the **Width** slider to set the extent to which the "alpha" blending is applied inside the cutout edge.

3. (Optional) Adjust the **Blur** slider to smooth out the cutout edge.

To create a vector-cropped bitmap:

1. Select **Vector-cropped Bitmap** from the **Output Type** drop-down menu.

2. (Optional) Drag the **Feather** slider to apply a soft or blurry edge inside the cutout edge.

3. (Optional) Drag the **Smoothness** slider to smooth out the cutout edge.

4. (Optional) The **Inflate** slider acts as an positive or negative offset from the cutout edge.

Selecting areas to keep or discard

A pair of brushes for keeping and discarding is used to enable parts of the image to be selected. The tools are called **Keep Brush** and **Discard Brush**, and are either used independently or, more typically, in combination with each other. When using either tool, the brush paints an area contained by an outline which is considered to be discarded or retained (depending on brush type). A configurable number of pixels adjacent to the outline area are blended.

> Either tool allows the default brush size to be set before you select areas for keeping/discarding. You can set your own custom size or use a small, medium, or large preset brush size. Choose from the top of the Studio workspace.

To aid the selection operation, several display modes are available to show selection.

Show Original, **Show Tinted**, and **Show Transparent** buttons respectively display the image with:

- selection areas only

- various coloured tints aiding complex selection operations

- checkerboard transparency areas marked for discarding.

For Show tinted, a red tint indicates areas to be discarded; a green tint shows areas to be kept.

For Show transparent mode, a different **Background colour** can be set (at bottom of the Studio) which might help differentiate areas to keep or discard.

To select image areas for keeping/discarding:

1. In Image Cutout Studio, click either   **Keep brush** or   **Discard brush** from the left of the Studio workspace.

2. (Optional) Pick a **Brush size** suitable for the area to be worked on.

3. (Optional) Set a **Grow tolerance** value to automatically expand the selected area under the cursor (by detecting colours similar to those within the current selection). The greater the value the more the selected area will grow.

4. Using the circular cursor, click and drag across the area to be retained. It's OK to repeatedly click and drag until your selection area is made—you can't lose your selection unless you click the **Reset** button. The **Undo** button reverts to the last made selection.

5. If you're outputting an alpha-edged bitmap, you can refine the area to be kept/discarded within Image Cutout Studio (only after previewing) with Erase and Restore touch-up tools. Vector-cropped images can be cropped using standard PagePlus crop tools outside of the Studio.

> Make your outline edge as exact as possible by using brush and touch-up tools before committing your work.

6. Click **OK** to create your cutout.

You'll see your image in its original location, but with the selected areas cut away (made transparent).

Refining your cutout area (alpha-edged bitmaps only)

If a vector-cropped image is created via Image Cutout Studio it's possible to subsequently manipulate the crop outline using crop tools. However, for alpha-edged bitmaps, Erase and Restore touch-up tools can be used to refine the cutout area within the Studio before completing your cutout. The latter can't be edited with crop tools.

> ● The touch-up tools are brush based and are only to be used to fine-tune your almost complete cutout—use your Keep and Discard brush tools for the bulk of your work!

To restore or remove portions of your cutout:

1. With your cutout areas already defined, click the **Preview** button (Output settings tab). You can use the button to check your cutout as you progress.

2. Click the   **Restore Touch-up Tool** or   **Erase Touch-up Tool** button from the left of the Studio workspace.

3. Paint the areas for restoring or erasing as you would with the brush tools.

4. Click **OK**.

> ✏ If you've worked on part of your image between each preview, you'll be asked if you want to save or discard changes.

Drawing and editing lines

PagePlus provides **Pencil**, **Straight Line**, **Pen**, and **QuickShape** tools for creating simple graphics.

Using the **line tools** (found on the Tools toolbar, on the Line flyout), you can draw single lines, connect line segments together, or join line ends to **close** the line, creating a **shape** (see Drawing and editing shapes on p. 169 for details). Use the Pointer Tool and the Curve context toolbar to resize or reshape lines once you've drawn them

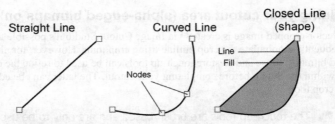

Straight Line   Curved Line   Closed Line (shape)

Line
Fill

Nodes

 The **Pencil Tool** lets you sketch curved lines and shapes in a freeform way.

 The **Straight Line Tool** is for drawing straight lines (for example, drawn in the column gutter to separate columns); rules at the top and/or bottom of the page; or horizontal lines to separate sections or highlight headlines.

 The **Pen Tool** lets you join a series of line segments (which may be curved or straight) using "connect the dots" mouse clicks.

Drawing lines

To draw a freeform line (with the Pencil Tool):

1. Choose the **Pencil Tool** from the Tools toolbar's Line flyout.

2. Click where you want the line to start, and hold the mouse button down as you draw. The line appears immediately and follows your mouse movements.

3. To end the line, release the mouse button. The line will automatically smooth out using a minimal number of nodes.

4. To extend the line, position the cursor over one of its red end nodes. The cursor changes to include a plus symbol. Click on the node and drag to add a new line segment.

To draw a straight line (with the Straight Line Tool):

1. Choose the ⟍ **Straight Line Tool** from the Tools toolbar's Line flyout.

2. Click where you want the line to start, and drag to the end point. The line appears immediately.

> To constrain the angle of the straight line to 15-degree increments, hold down the **Shift** key as you drag. (This is an easy way to make exactly vertical or horizontal lines.)

3. To extend the line, position the cursor over one of its red end nodes. The cursor changes to include a plus symbol. Click on the node and drag to add a new line segment.

To draw one or more line segments (with the Pen Tool):

1. Choose the 🖊 Pen Tool from the Tools toolbar's Line flyout. On the Curve Creation context toolbar, three buttons let you select which kind of segment to draw:

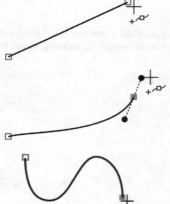

A **Straight** segment is simply a straight line connecting two nodes. (**Shortcut:** Press **1**)

A **Bézier** segment is curved, displaying control handles for precise adjustment. (**Shortcut:** Press **2**)

Smart segments appear without visible control handles, using automatic curve-fitting to connect each node. They are especially useful when tracing around curved objects and pictures. (**Shortcut:** Press **3**)

2. Select a segment type, then click where you want the line to start:

- For a **Straight** segment, click again (or drag) for a new node where you want the segment to end. **Shift**-click to align the segment at 15-degree intervals (useful for quick right-angle junctions).

- For a **Bézier** segment, click again for a new node and drag out a **control handle** from it. Click again where you want the segment to end, and a curved segment appears. The finished segment becomes selectable.

- For a **Smart** segment, click again for a new node. The segment appears as a smooth, best-fitting curve (without visible control handles) between the new node and the preceding node. Before releasing the mouse button, you can drag to "flex" the line as if bending a piece of wire. If the preceding corner node on the line is also smart, flexibility extends back to the preceding segment. You can **Shift**-click to create a new node that lines up at 15-degree intervals with the previous node.

3. To extend an existing line, repeat Step 2 for each new segment. Each segment can be of a different type.

4. To end the line, press **Esc**, double-click, or choose a different tool.

Curve context toolbar

The **Curve context toolbar** appears when you select a line or closed shape, and provides a variety of adjustment controls—including adding/deleting nodes and manipulation of curves.

See PagePlus help for information on editing lines.

Setting line properties

All lines, including those that enclose shapes, have numerous properties, including colour, weight (width or thickness), scaling, cap (end) and join (corner). You can vary these properties for any freehand, straight, or curved line, as well as for the outline of a shape. Note that text frames, tables, and artistic text objects have line properties, too.

To change line properties of a selected object:

- Use the Swatches tab to change the line's colour and/or shade. (If changing the outline colour of a shape or other object, click the **Line** button so that the line, not the fill, will change.) Click a gallery sample in the tab's Publication palette or one of the categorized palettes to apply that colour to the selected object. Alternatively, use the Colour tab to apply a colour to the selected object from a colour mixer.

- Use the Line tab or Line context toolbar (shown when a line is selected) to change the line's weight (thickness), type, or other properties. Select a line width, and use the drop-down boxes to pick the type of line. The context toolbar can also adjust line-end scaling as a percentage.

On the **Line** tab or context toolbar, the middle **Line Styles** drop-down menu provides the following styles: **None**, **Single**, **Calligraphic**, and several **Dashed** and **Double** line styles as illustrated below.

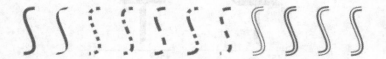

Several techniques offer additional ways to customize lines:

For dashed lines, select from one of five **Dashed** line styles (see above).

OR

(Tab only) Drag the **Dash Pattern** slider to set the overall pattern length (the number of boxes to the left of the slider) and the dash length (the number of those boxes that are black). The illustrations below show lines with pattern and dash lengths of (1) 4 and 2, and (2) 5 and 4:

For double lines, select from one of four **Double** line styles (see above).

(Tab only) For Calligraphic lines of variable width (drawn as if with a square-tipped pen held at a certain angle), select the calligraphic line style (opposite) from the drop-down menu then use the **Calligraphic Angle** box to set the angle of the pen tip, as depicted in the examples below.

The **Line** tab also lets you vary a line's **Cap** (end) and the **Join** (corner) where two lines intersect. Both properties are more conspicuous on thicker lines; joins are more apparent with more acute angles. The respective button icons clearly communicate each setting:

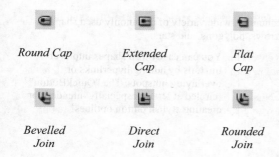

Round Cap   *Extended*   *Flat*
              Cap   *Cap*

Bevelled   *Direct*   *Rounded*
Join   *Join*   *Join*

To access all Line properties:

- Click the   **Line/Border** button on the Attributes toolbar's Fill flyout.

  In the **Line and Border** dialog, the **Line** tab lets you adjust all line properties as described above plus line end scaling (see PagePlus help for more information).

  > The **Border** tab (see Adding borders) provides a variety of other options for decorative outlines.

- To apply a border to specific edges of the object, use the dialog's **Border Edges** tab.

Drawing and editing shapes

PagePlus provides Pencil, Straight Line, Pen and QuickShape tools for creating simple graphics. **QuickShapes** are pre-designed objects that you can instantly add to your page, then adjust and vary using control handles. Another way to create a shape is to draw a line (or series of line segments) and then connect its start and end nodes, creating a **closed shape**. Once you've drawn a shape, you can adjust its properties—for example, apply gradient or bitmap fills (including your own bitmap pictures!) or apply transparency effects. You can even use sliding handles to create variations on the original QuickShape.

It's also possible to use the always-at-hand QuickShape context toolbar situated above the workspace to swap QuickShapes, and adjust a QuickShape's line weight, colour, style, and more. New shapes always take the default line and fill (initially a black line with no fill).

QuickShapes

The QuickShape flyout contains a wide variety of commonly used shapes, including boxes, ovals, arrows, polygons, and stars.

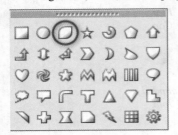

You can easily turn shapes into Web **buttons** by adding hyperlinks or overlaying hotspots. The "QuickButton" (circled at left) is especially intended for creating stylish button outlines!

To create a QuickShape:

1. Click the **QuickShape** button on the Tools toolbar and select a shape from the flyout. The button takes on the icon of the shape selected.

2. Click on the page to create a new shape at a default size. Drag to adjust its dimensions.

3. When the shape is the right size, release the mouse button. Now you can alter the shape by dragging on its handles.

To draw a constrained shape (such as a circle):

- Hold down the **Shift** key as you drag.

All QuickShapes can be positioned, resized, rotated, and filled. What's more, you can morph them using adjustable sliding handles around the QuickShape. Each shape changes in a logical way to allow its exact appearance to be altered.

To adjust the appearance of a QuickShape:

1. Click on the QuickShape to reveal one or more sliding handles around the shape. These are distinct from the "inner" selection handles. Different QuickShapes have different handles which have separate functions.

2. To change the appearance of a QuickShape, drag its handles.

> ▮ To find out what each handle does for a particular shape, move the Pointer Tool over the handle and read the HintLine.

Closed shapes

As soon as you draw or select a line, you'll see the line's nodes appear. Nodes show the end points of each segment in the line. Freehand curves typically have many nodes; straight or curved line segments have only two. You can make a shape by extending a line back to its starting point.

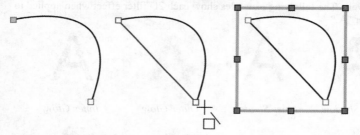

To turn a selected line into a shape:

- Select the line with the **Pointer Tool** and then click the ⊦⁺⊦ **Close Curve** button on the Curve context toolbar.

You can go the other way, too—break open a shape in order to add one or more line segments.

To break open a line or shape:

1. With the **Pointer** Tool, select the node where you want to break the shape.

2. Click the ⊦⁺⊦ **Break Curve** button on the Curve context toolbar. A line will separate into two lines. A shape will become a line, with the selected node split into two nodes, one at each end of the new line.

3. You can now use the **Pointer** tool to reshape the line as needed.

See online Help for more information on editing shapes.

Applying 2D filter effects

PagePlus provides a variety of **filter effects** that you can use to transform any object. "3D" filter effects let you create the impression of a textured surface and are covered elsewhere (see p. 175). Here we'll look at 2D filter effects exclusively. The following examples show each 2D filter effect when applied to the letter "A."

| *Drop Shadow* | *Inner Shadow* | *Outer Glow* | *Inner Glow* |

| *Inner Bevel* | *Outer Bevel* | *Emboss* | *Pillow Emboss* |

| *Gaussian Blur* | *Zoom Blur* | *Radial Blur* | *Motion Blur* |

| *Colour Fill* | *Feather* | *Outline* | *Reflection* |

PagePlus additionally provides the Shadow Tool for applying a shadow to an object directly on your page. Control handles let you adjust shadow blur, opacity and colour.

To apply 2D filter effects:

1. Select an object and click the *fx* **Filter Effects** button on the Attributes toolbar.

2. To apply a particular effect, check its box in the list at left.

3. To adjust the properties of a specific effect, select its name and vary the dialog controls. Adjust the sliders or enter specific values to vary the combined effect. (You can also select a slider and use the keyboard arrows.) Options differ from one effect to another.

4. Click **OK** to apply the effect or **Cancel** to abandon changes.

Creating reflections

A simple way to add creative flair to your page is to apply a vertical reflection on a selected object. The effect is especially eye-catching when applied to pictures, but can be equally impressive on artistic text, such as page titles or text banners. A combination of settings can control reflection height, opacity, offset and blurring.

Creating outlines

PagePlus lets you create a coloured outline around objects, especially text and shapes (as a **filter effect**). For any outline, you can set the outline width, colour fill, transparency, and blend mode. The outline can also take a gradient fill, a unique **contour** fill (fill runs from the inner to outer edge of the outline width), or pattern fill and can also sit inside, outside, or be centred on the object edge.

As with all effects you can switch the outline effect on and off. You'll be able to apply a combination of 2D or 3D filter effects along with your outline, by checking other options in the Filter Effects dialog.

Blur

Various blur effects can be applied to PagePlus objects. The types of blur include:

- **Gaussian**: the effect smoothes by averaging pixels using a weighted curve.

- **Zoom**: applies converging streaks to the image to simulate a zoom lens.

- **Radial**: applies concentric streaks to the object to simulate a rotating camera or subject.

- **Motion**: applies straight streaks to the object to simulate the effect of camera or subject movement.

Using the Shadow Tool

Shadows are great for adding flair and dimension to your work, particularly to pictures and text objects, but also to shapes, text frames and tables. To help you create them quickly and easily, PagePlus provides the **Shadow Tool** on the Attributes toolbar. The tool affords freeform control of the shadow effect allowing creation of adjustable **basic** or **skewed edge-based shadows** for any PagePlus object.

Basic (left) and skewed shadows (right) applied
to a basic square QuickShape

Adjustment of shadow colour, opacity, blur, and scaling/distance is possible using controllable nodes directly on the page (or via a supporting Shadow context toolbar). Nodes can be dragged inwards or outwards from the shadow origin to modify the shadow's blur and opacity. For a different colour, pick a new colour from the Colour or Swatches tab while the tool is selected. Depending on if a basic or skewed shadow is required, the origin can exist in the centre (shown) or at the edge of an object, respectively. You can change the shadow type at any time from the context toolbar.

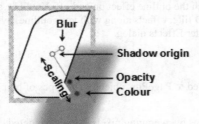

Once you've created a shadow, you can also fine-tune it as needed using the Filter Effects dialog.

Using 3D filter effects

3D filter effects go beyond 2D filter effects (such as shadow, glow, bevel, and emboss effects) to create the impression of a textured surface on the object itself. You can use the **Filter Effects** dialog to apply one or more effects to the same object. Keep in mind that none of these 3D effects will "do" anything to an unfilled object—you'll need to have a fill there to see the difference they make!

Overview

To apply a 3D filter effect to a selected object:

1. Click the **_fx_** **Filter Effects** button on the Attributes toolbar.

2. Check the **3D Effects** box at the left. The **3D Lighting** box is checked by default.

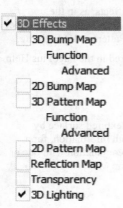

- **3D Effects** is a master switch for this group, and its settings of **Blur** and **Depth** make a great difference; you can click the "+" button to unlink them for independent adjustment.

- **3D Lighting** provides a "light source" without which any depth information in the effect wouldn't be visible. The lighting settings let you illuminate your 3D landscape and vary its reflective properties.

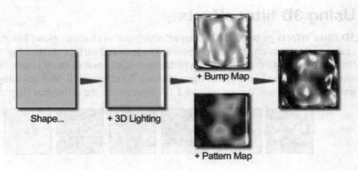

You'll notice that Bump Maps and Pattern Maps come in two varieties: "2D" and "3D." They are all three-dimensional effects-the 2D/3D distinction refers to how each one achieves its result. With the "2D map" variants, you begin by selecting a bitmap from a gallery. With the "3D" Bump Maps and Pattern Maps, you first pick a mathematical function. The function-based maps include data about the interior of the "space," while the bitmap-based maps describe only surface characteristics.

Multiple effects. You can combine multiple 3D filter effects, as in the illustration above. The effects are applied cumulatively, in a standard "pipeline" sequence: 3D Bump OR 2D Bump > 3D Pattern > 2D Pattern > 3D Lighting.

The procedures for applying 3D Filter Effects are covered in the PagePlus Help but here's a quick review of each effect type.

3D Bump Map

The **3D Bump Map** effect creates the impression of a textured surface by applying a mathematical function you select to add depth information, for a peak-and-valley effect. You can use 3D Bump Map in conjunction with one or more additional 3D filter effects-but not with a 2D Bump Map.

2D Bump Map

The **2D Bump Map** effect creates the impression of a textured surface by applying a greyscale bitmap you select to add depth information, for a peak-and-valley effect. You can use 2D Bump Map in conjunction with one or more additional 3D filter effects-but not with a 3D Bump Map.

3D Pattern Map

The **3D Pattern Map** effect creates the impression of a textured surface by applying a mathematical function you select to introduce colour variations. You can use 3D Pattern Map in conjunction with one or more other 3D filter effects.

2D Pattern Map

The **2D Pattern Map** effect creates the impression of a textured surface by applying a greyscale bitmap you select to introduce colour variations. You can use 2D Pattern Map in conjunction with one or more other 3D filter effects.

Transparency

The uniform transparency of an object (with 3D filter effects applied) can be controlled via the Transparency tab (see first example below). However, for more sophisticated transparency control, especially for simulating reflective lighting effects on glass objects, transparency settings can instead be set within the 3D filter effects dialog (check the **Transparency** option). Transparency can be adjusted independently for both non-reflective surfaces (typically an object's edge shadows shown when side-lit) and top-lit surfaces (see second example below).

50% Transparency   Filter Effect Transparency

3D Reflection Map

The **3D Reflection Map** effect is used to simulate mirrored surfaces by selection of a pattern (i.e., a bitmap which possesses a shiny surface) which "wraps around" a selected object. Patterns which simulate various realistic indoor and outdoor environments can be adopted, with optional use of 3D lighting to further reflect off object edges.

3D Lighting

The **3D Lighting** effect works in conjunction with other 3D effects to let you vary the surface illumination and reflective properties.

Applying a mesh warp envelope

Mesh warping lets you apply a Preset warp envelope to your PagePlus object (below) or modify a flexible grid of points and lines that you can drag to deform or distort an object and (optionally) its fill.

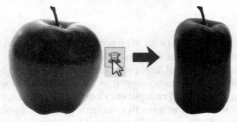

After applying a preset envelope from the Attributes toolbar's **Mesh Warp** flyout (or context toolbar), you can use the **Mesh Warp** context toolbar to switch the warp on/off, edit the mesh by varying its curvature and even custom-design a mesh to match a particular object's geometry—for example, curves that follow the facial contours in a bitmap image—for more precise control of the warp effect. The effect is removable and doesn't permanently alter the object.

The process of editing mesh warps and their envelopes is described in greater detail in the PagePlus Help.

Adding dimensionality (Instant 3D)

Using the **Instant 3D** feature, you can easily transform flat shapes (shown) and text into three-dimensional objects.

PagePlus provides control over 3D effect settings such as:

- **bevelling**: use several rounded and chiselled presets or create your own with a custom bevel profile editor.

- **lighting**: up to eight editable and separately coloured lights can be positioned to produce dramatic lighting effects.

- **lathe effects**: create contoured objects (e.g., a bottle cork) with the custom lathe profile editor and extrusion control.

- **texture**: control how texture is extruded on objects with non-solid fills.

- **viewing**: rotate your object in three dimensions.

- **material**: controls the extent to which lighting has an effect on the object's surfaces (great for 3D artistic text!).

An always-at-hand 3D context toolbar hosted above your workspace lets you configure the above settings—each setting contributes to the 3D effect applied to the selected object. For on-the-page object control you can transform in 3D with use of a red orbit circle, which acts as an axis from which you can rotate around the X-, Y-, and Z-axes in relation to your page. Look for the cursor changing as you hover over the red circles' nodes or wire frame.

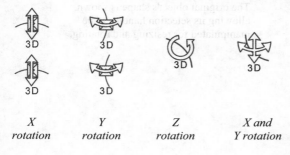

| *X* | *Y* | *Z* | *X and* |
| *rotation* | *rotation* | *rotation* | *Y rotation* |

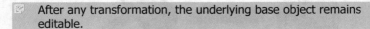

Transform about your 3D objects' axes instead of your pages' axes by holding the **Ctrl**-key down as you transform using the nodes.

You can also adjust the angle and elevation of each "active" light on the page by dragging the light pointer to a position which simulates a light source.

After any transformation, the underlying base object remains editable.

To add dimensionality:

1. Select an object and click the **Instant 3D** button on the Attributes toolbar (or choose **Instant 3D...** from the Format menu). The object immediately adopts 3D characteristics with a red orbit circle displayed in the object's foreground.

2. Click a 3D effect category from the first drop-down menu on the 3D context toolbar; the bar's options change dynamically according to the category currently selected. See the PagePlus Help for more details.

If you're not happy with how your 3D object is looking, you can revert to the object's initial transformation by either clicking the **Reset Defaults** button on the context toolbar or the **Instant 3D** button on the Attributes toolbar.

To switch off 3D effects:

- Click the **Remove 3D** button on the context toolbar. You can always click the Attribute toolbar's **Instant 3D** button at any time later to reinstate the effect.

To edit base properties of a 3D object:

- Select the 3D object, then click the **Edit** button at the bottom right-hand corner of the 3D object, i.e.

The original object's shape is shown, allowing its selection handles to be manipulated for resizing and rotating.

Using object styles

Object styles benefit your design efforts in much the same way as text styles and colour schemes. Once you've come up with a set of attributes that you like—properties like line colour, fill, border, and so on—you can save this cluster of attributes as a named style. PagePlus remembers which objects are using that style, and the style appears in the Styles tab , and can subsequently be applied to new objects. For example a Quick Star can have a stone effect applied via an object style you've saved previously (all object styles use a cog shape as the default object preview type).

Here's how object styles work to your advantage:

- Each object style can include settings for a host of object attributes, such as line colour, line style, fill, transparency, filter effects, font, and border. The freedom to include or exclude certain attributes, and the nearly unlimited range of choices for each attribute, makes this a powerful tool in the designer's arsenal.

- Any time you want to alter some aspect of a style (for example, change the line colour), you simply change the style definition. Instantly, all objects in your publication sharing that style update accordingly.

- Object styles you've saved globally appear not only in the original publication but in any new publication, so you can reuse exactly the same attractive combination of attributes for any subsequent design effort.

The Styles tab ships with multiple galleries of pre-designed styles that you can apply to any object, or customize to suit your own taste! Galleries exist in effect categories such as Blurs, 3D, Edge, Warp, Shadows, and more, with each category having further subcategories.

To apply an object style to one or more objects:

1. Display the **Styles** tab.

2. Expand the drop-down menu to select a named style category (e.g., Blurs), then pick a subcategory by scrolling the lower window.

3. Preview available styles as thumbnails (cog shapes are shown by default) in the window.

4. Click a style thumbnail in the panel to apply it to the selected object(s).
   OR
   Drag and drop the thumbnail onto any object.

The Object Style Manager can be used to add or delete categories or subcategories. You can even change the display order of categories, subcategories or thumbnails themselves.

To add, remove, and reorder style categories:

1. Select the tab's ▷ **Tab Menu** button and choose **Object Style Manager...** from the flyout menu.

2. Use the Add, Remove, Up, or Down buttons as appropriate in each window.

To remove an object style from a gallery:

- Right-click the thumbnail and choose **Delete**.

To unlink an object from its style definition:

- Right-click the object and choose **Format>Object Style>Unlink**.

If you've applied a style to an object but have lost track of the thumbnail—or want to confirm which style is actually being used on an object—you can quickly locate the thumbnail from the object.

To locate an object's style in the Styles tab:

- Right-click the object and choose **Format>Object Style>Locate in Studio**.

The Styles tab displays the gallery thumbnail for the object's style.

Normally, a publication's object styles are just stored locally—that is, as part of that publication; they don't automatically carry over to new publications. If you've created a new style you'll want to use in another publication, you can save it globally so that it will appear in the Styles tab each time you open a new publication.

To save a publication's object styles globally:

- Choose **Save Object Styles** from the Tools menu.

Saving Object Styles

To create a new object style based on an existing object's attributes:

1. Right-click the object and choose **Format>Object Style>Create**.

   The Style Attributes Editor dialog appears, with a tree listing object attributes on the left and a preview region on the right.

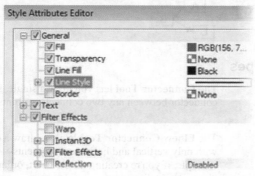

2. Click to expand or collapse sections within the attributes tree. Check any attributes you want to include in the style definition, and uncheck any you don't want to include.

3. If you want to change any of the current object settings, double-click an attribute (or select it and click the **Edit** button). This will bring up a detailed dialog for the particular attribute.

4. The **Object** pane in the preview region shows the currently selected object after applying the defined style. Select the **Artistic Text** or **Frame Text** tab to see the style applied to sample objects of those types.

5. Click the **Browse...** button to select the gallery category where you want to locate the style thumbnail , and optionally, save to a different Preview Type (Rounded Rectangle, Frame Text, or Artistic Text) instead of the default cog shape.

6. Type a name to identify the gallery thumbnail.

7. Click **OK**. A thumbnail for the new object style appears in the designated gallery.

Once an object style is listed in a gallery, you can modify it or create a copy (for example, to define a derivative style) by right-clicking on its thumbnail and choosing **Edit...** or **Copy...**.

Using connectors

Two Connector tools let you create dynamic link lines between any two objects. These connectors remain anchored to the objects, even if either or both of them are moved or resized. So, for example, it's easy to create a flow chart with connectors between boxes, then freely rearrange the layout while preserving the directional relationships!

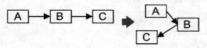

Connector types

The **Connector Tool** lets you draw a single, straight-line connector between any two connection points.

The **Elbow Connector Tool** lets you draw a connector with only vertical and horizontal segments—for example, if you're creating a flow chart, organization chart, or tree diagram.

Connection points

To make connections easy, each PagePlus object has default connection points, displayed whenever you select a Connector tool and hover over a target object. These default points (which can't be moved or deleted) are normally evenly distributed around an object's shape.

To create a connector:

1. For a straight-line connector, select the **Connector Tool** on the Connector Tools flyout (Tools toolbar).
    OR

    For an elbow connector, select the **Elbow Connector Tool** from the same location.

2. Either:

- Hover over an object so that default **connection points** become visible, e.g. for various shapes.

   OR

- Hover over an object's edge until you see a red square.

3. Drag from the object's connection point to another object's connection point (default or custom). Release the mouse button when the pointer is over the target connection point. A direct connector will appear between the two connection points.

Instead of using an object's default connection points, you can create your own custom connection points by either hovering over any shape's edge and dragging from that originating point or by simply creating a custom connection point with the Connection Point Tool. They can also be placed anywhere on the page, and are especially useful when creating a connection onto grouped QuickShapes or more complex grouped objects such as symbols.

To add a custom connection point (with tool):

1. Select an object.

2. Select the ⊠ **Connection Point Tool** on the Connector Tools flyout (Tools toolbar).

3. Click at a chosen location to place the custom connection point (inside or outside the object). The custom connection point appears in blue.

To view the connection points again you have to hover over the object which was selected while the connection point was created. Remember to enable either the Connector Tool or Elbow Connector Tool in advance.

Editing connection points and connectors

- ☒ To move a custom connection point, select the object to which it is associated and drag the point with the **Connection Point Tool**.

- ☒ To delete a custom connection point you've added, use the **Connection Point Tool** to click the object to which the connection point was associated, click the connection point you want to delete, and then press Delete. Default nodes are fixed and can't be deleted.

- ▶ To move, reshape, or detach/reattach a connector, use the **Pointer Tool** to drag individual nodes. Drag the end node of a connector to detach or reattach it. (See Drawing and editing lines on p. 163).

> If you draw a connector with either or both ends unconnected, the free ends stay anchored to the page as drawn. Of course, you can still move, reattach, or edit the connector just as if it were connected to an object.

As any connector is treated as an ordinary line, you can format it to add arrows, feathers, or other decorative line end.

To format the connecting line:

- To change the line properties, select the connector and display the Line tab. Use the controls to set line thickness, line end, and line dash pattern (see Setting line properties on p. 167).

- To change the line colour, use the Colour tab or Swatches tab (see Applying solid fills on p. 189).

- PagePlus lets you scale the connector's line ends in relation to the thickness of the line itself. Choose a **Line end scale** percentage value from the Connectors context toolbar (or go to **End scale** from **Format>Line and Border**). By default, line ends are included as part of the line length (**Internal line ends** option).

Colour, Fills, and Transparency

Colour, Fills, and
Transparency

Applying solid fills

PagePlus offers a number of ways to apply solid colour fills to objects of different kinds:

- You can apply solid colours to an object's **line** or **fill**. As you might expect, QuickShapes and closed shapes (see Drawing and editing shapes on p. 169) have both line and fill properties, whereas straight and freehand lines have only a line property.

- Characters in text objects can have fill colour or highlight colour. Text frames and table cells can have a background fill independent of the characters they contain.

- You can colourize a paint-type (bitmap) picture—that is, recolour it to use a different colour. If you recolour a full-colour picture, the colours will convert to tints or shades of the specified colour. You can also apply tinting to a full-colour picture to produce a low-intensity picture (useful for backgrounds behind text).

You can use the Colour tab, Swatches tab or a dialog box to apply solid colours to an object.

To apply a solid colour via the Colour tab:

1. Select the object(s) or highlight a range of text.

2. Click the **Colour** tab and select one of several colour modes (RGB, CMYK, or HSL) from the drop-down list.

3. Click the ⬓ **Fill**, ⬚ **Line**, or **A** **Text** button at the top of the tab to determine where colour will be applied. The colour of the underline reflects the colour of your selected object.

4. Select a colour from the colour spectrum or sliders depending on colour mode selected.

To apply a solid colour via the Swatches tab:

1. Select the object(s) or highlight a range of text.

2. Click the **Swatches** tab.

3. Click the ⬚ **Fill**, ▬ **Line**, or **A** **Text** button at the top of the tab to determine where colour will be applied.

4. Select a colour swatch from the **Publication palette** (commonly used colours and those previously applied to your publication) or Standard **Palette** (supplied preset swatches).

Use **Format>Fill...** to apply colour via a dialog.

To change a solid colour's shade/tint (lightness):

1. Select the object and set the correct Fill, Line or Text button in the Colour tab.

2. From the Colour mode drop-down menu, select **Tinting**.

3. Drag the Shade/Tint slider to the left or right to darken or lighten your starting colour, respectively (the original colour is set at 0%). You can also enter a percentage value in the box (entering 0 in the input box reverts to the original colour).

> 🔷 Adjust the `0%` ▶ percentage tinting via slider or direct input to apply object tinting from the Swatches tab.

PagePlus automatically adds used colours to the Publication Palette in the Swatches tab. This palette is loaded by default but instead you can view and adopt colours from a standard RGB, WebSafe, or selection of themed palettes by clicking the tab's **Palette** button. Colours can be added, edited or deleted from the Publication Palette but not from other palettes.

Working with gradient and bitmap fills

Gradient fills provide a gradation or spectrum of colours spreading between two or more points on an object. A gradient fill has an editable path with nodes that mark the origin of each of these key colours. A bitmap fill uses a named bitmap—often a material, pattern, or background image—to fill an object.

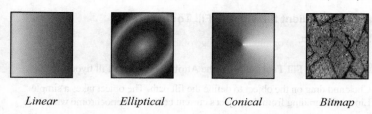

Linear   *Elliptical*   *Conical*   *Bitmap*

You can apply preset gradient and bitmap fills from the Swatches tab to shapes, text frames, table cells, and to any artistic, frame, and table text. Using the **Fill Tool** from the Attributes toolbar's Fill flyout (or from **Format>Fill**), you can vary the fill's path on an object for different effects (see PagePlus help).

Applying different transparency effects (using the **Transparency** tab) won't alter the object's fill settings as such, but may significantly alter a fill's actual appearance.

Applying a gradient or bitmap fill

There are several ways to apply a gradient or bitmap fill: using the Fill Tool, the **Swatches** tab, or a dialog.

The easiest way to apply a gradient or bitmap fill is to use one of a range of pre-supplied swatch thumbnails in the Swatches tab's **Gradient** or **Bitmap** palettes. The Fill Tool and a Fill dialog are alternative methods for creating gradient fills.

To apply a gradient or bitmap fill using the Swatches tab:

1. Click the Swatches tab and ensure the [🔲] **Fill** button is selected.
   Note that the colour of the underline reflects the colour of your selected object.

2. [🔲▾] For gradient fills, select a gradient category, e.g. Linear, Elliptical, etc., from the **Gradient** button's drop-down menu.
   OR
   [🔲▾] For bitmap fills, select a drop-down menu category from the **Bitmap** button.

3. Select the object(s), and then click the appropriate gallery swatch for the fill you want to apply.
   OR
   Drag from the gallery swatch onto any object and release the mouse button.

4. If needed, adjust the fill's **Tint** at the bottom of the tab with the tab slider or set a percentage value in the input box.

To apply a gradient fill with the Fill Tool:

1. Select an object.

2. Click the **Fill Tool** button on the Attributes toolbar's Fill flyout.

3. Click and drag on the object to define the fill path. The object takes a simple Linear fill, grading from the object's current colour to monochrome white, e.g.

Note: If the object is white already (or has no fill), grading is from white to black.

Alternatively, a dialog can be used to add or subtract **key colours** from the gradient, apply different key colours to individual nodes, or vary the overall shading of the effect applied to the object.

To apply or edit a gradient or bitmap fill using a dialog:

1. Right-click the object and choose **Format>Fill**, or select it and choose **Fill...** from the Format menu.
   OR

   Click the **Fill** button on the Attributes toolbar's Fill flyout.

2. Choose the fill type and the desired fill category. Note that you can also use the dialog to apply a solid fill.

   • For gradient fills, select **Gradient** from the **Type** drop-down menu, and pick a gradient preset. A two-colour gradient has two nodes, one at each end of its path.
     OR
     Click the **From** and **To** buttons to specify the gradient's start and end colours.
     OR
     Click the **Edit** button if you want to add or subtract key colours from the currently chosen gradient (see Editing the gradient fill spectrum below), apply different key colours to individual nodes, or vary the overall shading of the effect applied to the object. You can adjust the fill's shade/tint as needed using the drop-down list.

   • For bitmap fills, select **Bitmap** from the **Type** drop-down menu, choose a category, and then click a gallery swatch.

3. Click **OK** to apply the effect or fill to the object.

Editing the fill path

When you select a fillable object, the Fill tool becomes available (otherwise it's greyed out). If the object uses a **gradient fill**, you'll see the **fill path** displayed as a line, with nodes marking where the spectrum between each key colour begins and ends. Adjusting the node positions determines the actual spread of colours between nodes. You can also edit a gradient fill by adding, deleting, or changing key colours (see below).

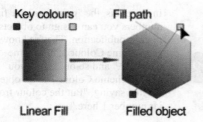

To adjust the gradient fill path on a selected object:

1. Click the ![Fill Tool icon] **Fill Tool** button on the Attributes toolbar's Fill flyout. The object's fill path appears.

2. Use the Fill tool to drag the start and end path nodes, or click on the object for a new start node and drag out a new fill path. The gradient starts where you place the start node, and ends where you place the end node.

Each gradient fill type has a characteristic path. For example, Linear fills have single-line paths, while Elliptical fills have a two-line path so you can adjust the fill's extent in two directions away from the centre. If the object uses a **bitmap fill**, you'll see the fill path displayed as two lines joined at a centre point. Nodes mark the fill's centre and edges.

Using schemes

In PagePlus, a **colour scheme** is a cluster of five complementary colours that you can apply to specific elements in one or more publications. The **Schemes** tab displays preset schemes which can be selected at any point during the design process. Each publication can have just one colour scheme at a time; the current scheme is highlighted in the **Schemes** tab. You can easily switch schemes, modify scheme colours, apply schemes to any publication, even create your own custom schemes. Colour schemes are saved globally, so the full set of schemes is always available.

How colour schemes work

Colour schemes in PagePlus work much like a paint-by-numbers system, where various regions of a layout are coded with numbers, and a specific colour is assigned (by number) to each region. For example, imagine a line drawing coded with the numbers 1 through 5. To fill it in, you'd use paint from jars also numbered 1 through 5. Swapping different colours into the paint jars, while keeping the numbers on the drawing the same, would produce quite a different painting.

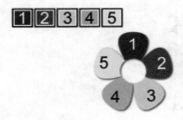

In PagePlus, the "paint jars" are five numbers you can assign to objects in your publication. They're known as "Scheme Colour 1," "Scheme Colour 2," and so on. When you apply Scheme Colour 1 to an object, it's like saying, "Put the colour from jar number 1 here."

- The **Schemes** tab shows the various available schemes, each with a different set of five colours in the five "jars." Whichever named colour scheme you select, that scheme's first colour (as shown in its sample) will appear in regions defined as Scheme Colour 1, its second colour will map to Scheme Colour 2, and so on throughout the publication.

The example below shows three different schemes as applied to a design that's been marked with Scheme Colours 1 through 5 as in the example above.

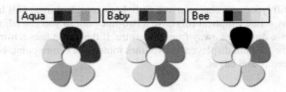

To select a colour scheme:

1. Click the **Schemes** tab. The currently assigned scheme is highlighted in the list.

2. Click a different colour scheme sample. Objects in the publication that have been assigned one of the five colour scheme numbers (see below) are updated with the corresponding colour from the new scheme.

You can repeat this selection process indefinitely. When you save a publication, its current colour scheme is saved along with the document.

Applying scheme colours to objects

If you create new elements in a publication to which you have applied a colour scheme, or start a publication from scratch, how can you extend the current colour scheme to the new objects? Although you'll need to spend some time working out which colour combinations look best, the mechanics of the process are simple. Recalling the paint-by-numbers example above, all you need to do is assign one of the five current scheme colour numbers to an object's line and/or fill.

To assign a scheme colour to an object:

1. Select the object and choose a ⬛ **Fill**, ⬜ **Line**, or **A** **Text** button at the top of the Swatches tab depending on the desired effect.

2. From the bottom of the Swatches tab, click on the scheme colour that you want to apply to the fill, line, or text (or you can drag the colour instead).

If an object's fill uses a scheme colour, the corresponding sample in Swatches tab will be highlighted whenever the object is selected.

PagePlus lets you create your own colour scheme either from scratch or by modifying an existing scheme. See online Help for more information.

Modifying and creating colour schemes

If you've tried various colour schemes but haven't found one that's quite right, you can modify any of the colours in an existing scheme to create a new one, or create your own named scheme from scratch.

To modify or create a colour scheme:

1. Select **Scheme Manager...** from the Tools menu.
    OR
    Click on the ▶ **Tab Menu** button and choose from the drop-down menu.

    The **Scheme Manager** dialog appears, with the current scheme colours shown on the Edit tab.

2. To select a different scheme, switch to the dialog's **Schemes** tab and select a scheme in the scrolling list. Clicking **OK** at this point applies the scheme to the publication, or you can go back to the Edit tab and adjust scheme colours.

On the Edit tab, each of the five scheme colour numbers has its own drop-down list, showing available colours in the PagePlus palette. (Additionally, you'll see options for Web publishing scheme colours for Hyperlink, Followed Hyperlink, Active Hyperlink, Rollover Hyperlink, Background and On-page.)

3. To set or change a colour, simply click the adjacent button and select a new colour. Click **More Colours...** to display the Colour Selector.

4. To store the modified scheme in the Schemes tab, click **Save Scheme....** If modifying an existing scheme, leave the name unaltered. If creating a new scheme, enter a new name.

5. To apply the scheme to the current publication (or web site), click **OK**.

Managing publication palettes

Each PagePlus publication has a particular set of colours, known as a **palette**, which appear as a set of gallery swatches in the **Swatches** tab. PagePlus ships with a range of palettes, stored separately as files with the .PLT file extension (e.g., **RGB.plt**). New paper and Web publications initially use the standard RGB palette (you can change the default palette if you wish). You can modify a project's palette and create custom palettes as needed by adding, removing, or modifying palette colours. A publication's palette is always saved along with the PagePlus project and loaded when the project is opened.

Any new colours you create will automatically be added to the Swatches tab (in the **Publication palette**, which hosts other colours previously used in the current publication along with a selection of commonly used colours (e.g., Red, Green, Blue, etc.). Added colours are loaded back into the gallery when you reopen the publication. However, a publication can also include colours that aren't part of its palette, and hence don't appear in the Swatches tab. For example, you might apply a gallery colour to an object and then modify its shade/tint value, creating a unique colour. Any such colours are of course saved in the publication, but they remain separate from the palette itself unless you explicitly add them.

PagePlus lets you quickly load standard RGB, CMYK or "themed" palettes as well as save and load custom palettes for use in other publications.

To add a custom colour to the Publication palette automatically:

- RGB ▼ With the Colour tab selected, optionally choose a colour mode from the **Colour mode** drop-down list.

- Pick a colour from the displayed colour spectrum (or use colour sliders).
  OR

- Select the ✎ **Colour Picker** on the Colour tab to select any colour already on your page. Optionally, hold down the mouse button and drag the cursor onto the page to get a zoomed-in view of pixel colours.

- Don't colour pick with an object selected, otherwise you'll recolour the object with the picked up colour.

- You can also add or edit standard or "themed" palette colours to the Publication palette by right-clicking on a palette swatch then selecting the Add or Edit option, or by using the Palette Manager.

- If you don't want to add colours automatically, uncheck Automatically Add to Publication palette on the Colour tab's ▷ Tab Menu button.

To add an object's solid fill colour to the Publication palette:

- Right-click the object and choose **Format>Add Fill to Studio**. The colour is added to the Publication palette of the Swatches tab directly.

To edit a specific palette colour in the Publication palette:

1. Right-click a sample in the Publication palette of the Swatches tab and choose **Edit**.

2. Choose a different colour from the colour spectrum in the **Colour Selector** dialog.

3. Click the **OK** button. The colour is updated in the Publication palette.

To remove a colour from the publication's palette:

- Right-click on the colour in the Publication palette of the Swatches tab and choose **Delete**. Alternatively, use the Palette Manager.

To load a named palette:

1. In the Swatches tab, click the down arrow on the ▦ ▾ **Palette** button.

2. From the resulting drop-down menu, select a standard (e.g., standard cmyk or rgb) or "themed" palette.

The loaded palette's colours appear as swatches in the Swatches tab, replacing the swatches previously visible. Note that changing the palette has no effect on colours already defined for particular objects in your publication.

Using the Palette Manager and Colour Selector

The Palette Manager and Colour Selector are complementary dialogs.

- The **Palette Manager** extends the Colour Selector's Publication palette tab. It not only lets you modify the publication's current palette but also load and save named palettes.

- The **Colour Selector** lets you choose a colour to apply or mix custom colours. Its **Models** tab displays the colour space of several established colour models: RGB (red, green blue), HSL (hue, saturation, luminosity), CMYK (cyan, magenta, yellow, black), and PANTONE® Colours. For all colour models, the values are in the range of 0 to 255. Its **Publication palette** tab lets you modify and view the set of colours associated with the Publication palette.

To display the Palette Manager:

- Choose **Palette Manager...**from the Tools menu.

To add a PANTONE® colour to the publication's palette:

- Display the Palette Manager, select **New**, then in the Model list on the **Models** tab choose **PANTONE® Colours**.

PANTONE refers to Pantone, Inc.'s check-standard trademark for colour reproduction and colour reproduction materials. For details, see PagePlus help.

If you've added new colours to the palette and will want to use them in other publications, you can save the palette.

To save the Publication palette:

- In the Palette Manager, click **Save As...** and specify a name for the palette.

If the palette is saved to the dialog's default folder, the saved palette's name will appear in the drop-down menu of the **Palette** button (Swatches tab).

> Another option if you'll want to use the current palette in another publication is to use the Save Defaults command to record the colour settings globally, so they will be available whenever you create a new publication. For details, see Updating and saving defaults on p. 24.

Working with transparency

Transparency effects are great for highlights, shading and shadows, and simulating "rendered" realism. They can make the critical difference between flat-looking illustrations and images with depth and snap. PagePlus fully supports variable transparency and lets you apply gradient or bitmap transparencies to create your own 32-bit, anti-aliased images. You can export transparent graphics as GIFs, PNGs, or TIFs and preserve transparency effects in both your printed output and your Web pages.

Transparencies work rather like fills that use "disappearing ink" instead of colour. The more transparency in a particular spot, the more "disappearing" takes place there, and the more the object(s) underneath show through. Just as a gradient fill can vary from light to dark, a transparency can vary from more to less, i.e. from clear to opaque, as in the illustration:

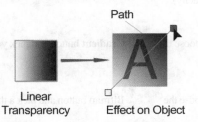

Path

Linear
Transparency

Effect on Object

In PagePlus, transparency effects work very much like greyscale fills. Just like fills...

- Transparency effects are applied from the Studio—in this case, using the Transparency tab.

- The Transparency tab's gallery has thumbnails in shades of grey, where the lighter portions represent more transparency. To apply transparency, you click thumbnails or drag them onto objects.

- Most transparency effects have a path you can edit—in this case, with the **Transparency Tool**.

As for the effects available on the Swatches tab, all are comparable to the fills of the same name:

- **Solid** transparency distributes the transparency equally across the object.

- **Gradient** transparencies include linear, elliptical, and conical effects (each thumbnail's tooltip identifies its category), ranging from clear to opaque.

- The **Bitmap** gallery includes texture maps based on the Swatches tab's selection of bitmaps.

Applying transparency

You can apply gradient and bitmap transparency from the Transparency tab to shapes, text frames, table cells, and to any artistic, frame, and table text. Using the Transparency Tool from the Attributes toolbar's Transparency flyout (or from **Format>Transparency**), you can vary the transparency's path on an object for different effects.

To apply transparency with Transparency tab:

1. With your object selected, go to the Transparency tab.

2. For solid transparency, select the ⬜ **Solid** button and pick a thumbnail from the solid transparency gallery. The lighter thumbnails represent more transparency (expressed as percentage Opacity).
   OR

   For gradient transparency, choose the ◤ **Gradient** button and pick your thumbnail.
   OR

   For bitmap transparency, choose the ⬜▾ **Bitmap** button and pick a thumbnail from a range of categories.

3. The transparency is applied to the object(s).

Alternatively, drag the desired thumbnail from the gallery to an object, and release the mouse button.

The process of editing gradient transparencies is the same as that for editing gradient fills.

The bitmap transparency type features its own gallery of preset "texture maps," based on the bitmap fills available on the Swatches tab. Adding bitmap transparencies to the gallery is the same as adding bitmap fills. You can create your own custom categories of bitmap transparency, which mirror those on the Swatches tab.

Changes to the Transparency gallery are recorded as global settings.

Setting the default transparency

The **default transparency** means the transparency that will be applied to the next new object you create. Local defaults only affect objects in the current project. For information on setting defaults in PagePlus, see Updating and saving defaults on p. 24.

Printing your
Publication

Printing basics

PagePlus supports scaling, tiling, colour separations, and many other useful printing options. Here we'll cover what you need to know for basic desktop printer output. If you're working with a service bureau or professional printer and need to provide PostScript output, see Generating professional output (p. 207; which also covers PDF output for professional printing).

To set up your printer or begin printing:

* Click the 🖨 **Print** button on the Standard toolbar. The Print dialog appears.

To print:

1. On the **General** tab, select a printer from the list. If necessary, click the **Properties** button to set up the printer for the correct page size, etc.

2. If necessary, click the **Layout**, **Separations**, or **Prepress** tab(s) to set special print options.

   * To set options for scaling, thumbnails, multiple pages, tiling, or mail merge, select the **Layout** tab. For details, see Printing special formats on p. 205.

   * To specify settings for PostScript colour separations, select the **Separations** tab.

   * To set professional print options select the **Prepress** tab.

3. Select the print range to be printed, e.g. the whole document, the selection area, a specific page, or range of pages. PagePlus also lets you choose odd or even sheets to print, and also various double- or single-sided options that override your current Printer Property settings.

   If you're printing a book, you can select **Entire book** to output all chapters, or **Selected chapters** to output just those you selected. Whichever option you've chosen, a drop-down list lets you export all sheets in the range, or just odd or even sheets, with the option of printing in reverse order.

4. Select the number of copies.

5. The Preview window shows how your publication maps to the selected paper size. You can click the dialog's **Preview** button to hide and show the window.

6. Click **OK**.

Previewing the printed page

The **Print Preview** mode changes the screen view to display your layout without frames, guides, rulers, and other screen items. Special options, such as tiled output or crop marks, are not displayed. A **Trimmed Page mode** can be entered which is similar to Print Preview mode but lets you continue designing without layout aids having to be displayed.

To preview the printed page:

- Click the  **Print Preview** button on the Standard toolbar.

In Print Preview mode, the lower toolbar provides a variety of familiar view options, plus the **Multipage** button, which lets you preview your publication using a page array.

To arrange multiple pages in the preview window:

1. Click the 🔠 **Multisheet** button. An array selector appears.
2. Move the pointer across the menu to choose an array. To expand the number of choices, move the pointer upwards and to the right.

3. Click once to make your selection.

To return to single page view:

- Click the 🔠 **Multisheet** button and select the "1x1 Sheets" array.

To cancel Print Preview mode:

- Click the ❌ **Close** button.

Working in Trimmed Page Mode:

Trimmed Page Mode lets you toggle between the page you're currently working on (complete with visible guides, pasteboard objects, text marks, etc.) and a preview page which shows how your page will appear in print. PagePlus takes this useful feature a step further by allowing the page content to be edited whilst still in Trimmed Page mode.

To enter Trimmed Page mode:

- Click the ⬚ **Trimmed Page Mode** button on the Hintline toolbar.

Printing special formats

Printing booklets

PagePlus automatically performs **imposition** of folded publications when you use **File>Page Setup...** and select or define a **Folded Publications** type. The settings ensure that two or four pages of the publication are printed on each sheet of paper, with pages printed following the booklet sequence. This saves you from having to calculate how to position and collate pairs of pages on a single larger page, and lets you use automatic page numbering for the booklet pages.

To produce double-sided sheets, use your printer's double-sided option or run sheets through twice, printing first the front and then the back of the sheet (reverse top and bottom between runs). The sheets can then be collated and bound at their centre to produce a booklet, with all the pages in the correct sequence. With complex setups, you may wish to use commercial printing.

Printing posters and banners

Posters and banners are large-format publications where the page size extends across multiple sheets of paper. To have PagePlus take care of the printing, set up your publication beforehand using File/Page Setup... (with the **Large Publications** option) to preview and select a particular preset arrangement.

Even if the publication isn't set up as a poster or banner, you can use tiling and scaling settings (see "Tiling" below) to print onto multiple sheets from a standard size page. Each section or tile is printed on a single sheet of paper, and the various tiles can then be joined to form the complete page. To simplify arrangement of the tiles and to allow for printer margins, you can specify an overlap value.

Scaling

- Under "Special Printing" on the Print dialog's **Layout** tab, set the "As in document - % Scale factor" option to specify a custom scaling percentage. The default is 100% or normal size. To scale your work to be printed at a larger size, specify a larger value; to scale down, specify a smaller value. Check **Fit Many** to have PagePlus fit as many pages as possible on each sheet—for example, two A5 pages on a landscape A4 sheet.

- Set "Scale to fit paper size" values to adjust artwork automatically to fit neatly on the printed page.

- Note that the Fit Many option ignores printer margins, while Scale to Fit takes them into account. So if you use Fit Many, make sure your page layout borders don't extend beyond the printable region.

Printing thumbnails

- Under "Special Printing" on the Print dialog's **Layout** tab, set the "Print as thumbnails" option to print multiple pages at a reduced size on each printed sheet, taking printer margins into account. Specify the number of thumbnails per sheet in the value box.

PagePlus will print each page of the publication at a reduced size, with the specified number of small pages or "thumbnails" neatly positioned on each printed sheet.

Multiple pages

- Under "Multiple pages per Sheet" on the Print dialog's **Layout** tab, select an option.

The multiple page options are enabled when you are working with a page from the Small Publications category in Page Setup. You can select the number of times to repeat each page, and tell PagePlus to skip a certain number of regions on the first sheet of paper. Skipping regions is useful if, for example, you've already peeled off several labels from a label sheet, and don't want to print on the peeled-off sections. Check the Preview window to see how the output will look.

- If you haven't set up the publication as a Small Publication, but still want to print multiple pages per sheet, try using the **Fit Many** option (see "Scaling" above). Note that this option ignores printer margins and doesn't change the imposition (orientation) of output pages.

Tiling

- Under "Tiling" on the Print dialog's **Layout** tab, check the **Print tiled pages** option to print large (or enlarged) pages using multiple sheets of paper.

- Set the **% Scale factor** to print at a larger size (e.g. 300%).

Each section or tile is printed on a single sheet of paper; the various tiles can then be joined to form the complete page. Use this option for printing at larger sizes than the maximum paper size of your printer, typically for creating banners and posters. To simplify arrangement of the tiles and to allow for printer margins, you can specify an overlap value.

Generating professional output

Beyond printing your own copies on a desktop printer, or having copies photo-reproduced at a quick print shop, you may wish to consider professional (typically offset) printing. For example, if you need to reproduce more than about 500 copies of a piece, photocopying begins to lose its economic advantages. Or you may need **spot colour** or **process colour** printing for a particular job. You can output your PagePlus publication and hand it off to any trusted commercial printer.

If you're not using colour matching, we suggest you set up **ICC device profiles** for image colours and enable **colour management** so that images in the exported file include correct colour space information. You can also specify a device profile for your desktop printer for accurate on-screen proofing of desktop-printed colours. For details, see Managing screen and output colours.

Unless you're handing off camera-ready artwork, your print provider will specify the format in which you should submit the publication: either PDF/X or PostScript (see online Help). Once you've decided whether to output as PDF or PostScript, you'll need to set Prepress options before choosing the appropriate output command.

The Separation and Pre-press options are further described in the PagePlus Help. In addition, the process for producing colour separations is detailed.

PDF/X

PDF is a format developed by Adobe to handle documents in a device- and platform-independent manner. PDF excels as an electronic distribution medium and the reliable **PDF/X** formats are perfect for delivering a publication file to a professional printer. Your print partner can tell you whether to deliver PDF/X-1 or PDF/X-1a (PagePlus supports both)—but from the PagePlus end of things you won't see a difference. In either mode, all your publication's colours will be output in the CMYK colour space, and fonts you've used will be embedded.

A single PDF/X file will contain all the necessary information (fonts, images, graphics, and text) your print partner requires to produce either spot or process colour separations.

To output your publication as a PDF/X file:

1. Choose **Publish as PDF...** from the File menu.

2. Review General and Advanced tab settings (see Exporting PDF files).

When preparing a PDF/X file for professional printing, choose either "PDF X/1" or "PDF X/1a" in the General tab's **Compatibility** list, as advised by your print partner. Also inquire whether or not to **Impose pages**; this option is fine for desktop printing of a folded publication or one that uses facing pages, but a professional printer may prefer you to leave the imposition (page sequencing) to them.

3. Review Prepress tab settings.

You don't need to worry about the Compression or Security tabs; these only apply to standalone PDFs.

Manual duplex printing

Duplex (two-sided) printing can give your greetings cards and other documents the edge. It can also save money by allowing you to use less paper. However, not all printers have this built-in duplexing function and are considered **simplex** (supports single-sided printing only). Using the Manual Duplex Printing wizard, you can overcome this limitation of simplex printers by flipping pages in the printer's manual feed tray when prompted.

To set up your printer:

1. Go to **File>Setup Manual Duplex Printing...**

2. A list of printers available for manual duplex printing will be displayed. Select the printer that you wish to configure and click **Next**.

3. Ensure that the printer tray has paper loaded and click **Next**.

4. Follow the instructions and select the options that apply to your printout. Click **Next** when you are ready to proceed through the setup.

5. At the end of the configuration, you will be asked whether you would like an instruction page when using the manual duplex with this printer. If you select "yes" (recommended), an instruction sheet will be printed whenever you use the Manual Duplex option with this printer.

6. Click **Finish**.

> The instruction page can potentially save wasted time and money by helping to prevent the paper from being loaded incorrectly when it is reloaded into the printer. If at a later date you decide that you don't want the instruction page, you can turn it off by running through the Setup again.
>
> You must configure your printer before you can use the Manual Duplex printing option.

To print (using manual duplex):

1. Go to **File>Print...**

2. In the Print dialog, set your printing options and choose **Manual Duplex** printing from the **Double-sided options** drop-down menu.

3. Click **Print**.

4. The first set of pages should print along with an instruction page if you requested one. Place the paper back in the tray and press continue to print the other side.

5. You should now have a double-sided printout!

Saving print profiles

You can save the current combination of settings made in the Print dialog as a **print profile** with a unique name. Note that the profile includes settings from all tabs except the Separations tab. By the way, don't confuse these PagePlus "print profiles" with ICC "device profiles."

To save current print settings as a print profile:

- On the Print dialog's **General** tab, click the **Save As...** button next to the Print Profile list.

- Type in a new name and click **OK**.

The settings are saved as a file with the extension .ppr.

You can restore the profile later on simply by choosing its name in the list.

Publishing and Sharing

9

Exporting PDF files

PDF (short for Portable Document Format) is a cross-platform file format developed by Adobe. In a relatively short time, PDF has evolved into a worldwide standard for document distribution which works equally well for electronic or paper publishing—including professional printing. In recent years, print stores are moving away from PostScript and toward the newer, more reliable **PDF/X** formats expressly targeted for graphic arts and high quality reproduction. Several different "flavours" of PDF/X exist; PagePlus supports PDF/X-1 and PDF/X-1a.

To export your publication as a PDF file:

1. Prepare the publication following standard print publishing guidelines, and taking the distribution method into account.

2. (Optional) Insert hyperlinks as needed, for example to link table of contents entries to pages in the document.

3. (Optional) To create **pop-up annotations**, insert PageHints as needed.

4. (Optional) Once the publication is final, prepare a bookmark list (see Creating a PDF bookmark list on p. 214).
   Note: Bookmarks appear as a separate list in a special pane when the PDF file is viewed. They can link to a specific page or to an **anchor** (for example, a piece of text or a graphic object) in your publication.

5. Choose **Publish as PDF...** from the File menu and check your export settings. (To export the whole publication using default settings, you won't need to change any settings.) For a detailed explanation of each export setting see PagePlus Help.

6. Click **OK** to proceed to export.

If you checked **Preview PDF file in Acrobat**, the resulting PDF file appears in the version of Adobe Acrobat Reader installed on your system.

> You can insert sound and movie clips in your publication which will play in your exported PDF file, whether you've created a PDF slideshow, PDF form or a simple PDF document. Choose options from the PDF Media Clip> located on the Insert menu.

Creating a PDF bookmark list

Bookmarks are optional links that appear in a separate pane of the Adobe Reader when a PDF file is displayed. Typically, a bookmark links to a specific location such as a section heading in the publication, but it can also link to a document page. You can insert bookmarks by hand, or PagePlus can apply **automatic generation** to produce a nested bookmark list up to six levels deep, derived from named styles in your publication.

A **Bookmark Manager** enables you to view all your bookmarks at a glance, organize them into a hierarchy of entries and subentries, and create, modify or delete existing bookmarks as needed.

To use styles to automatically generate bookmarks:

1. Decide which named styles you want to designate as headings at each of up to six levels.

2. Check your publication to make sure these styles are used consistently.

3. Choose **Bookmark Manager...** from the Tools menu and click **Automatic...**.

In the dialog, you'll see a list of all the style names used in your publication.

4. Check boxes to include text of a given style as a heading at a particular level (1 through 6). For example, you could include all text using the "Heading" style as a first-level heading. To remove all bookmarks in the list, clear all check boxes.

5. Click **OK** to generate bookmarks.

The mechanics of **creating a PDF bookmark list by hand** are simple. For example, to create a basic list with bookmarks to section heads, you simply proceed forward through the publication, inserting a bookmark for each heading. Bookmarking a specific location (for example, a piece of text or a graphic object) entails placing an **anchor** at that location; the anchor serves as the target for the bookmark link.

To insert bookmarks by hand:

1. (Optional) To bookmark a specific location in the publication, first place the cursor at that point or select an object. You can select a range of text (for example, a section heading) to use it as the actual text of the bookmark.

2. Choose **Bookmark...** from the Insert menu (or **Insert Bookmark...** from the right-click menu).
   OR
   Choose **Bookmark Manager...** from the Tools menu. In the bookmark tree, display the entry below which you want to create the new bookmark. (Check **Create as sub-entry** if you want the new bookmark nested as a "child" of the selected entry.) Then click the **Create...** button.

3. In the Create Bookmark dialog, the **Text** field shows the range of text you selected if any (for example, a section heading). You can leave this if it's suitable for the bookmark text or edit it as needed; otherwise enter new text if the field is empty.

4. Click to select the bookmark destination type, then enter the destination.
   • To bookmark a specific location, choose **An anchor in your publication**. To place a new anchor at the cursor location, select **<Anchor at current selection>** from the list below. You'll be prompted to enter an anchor name (with the bookmark text as the default); edit the name if you like and click **OK**. To bookmark a previously placed anchor, simply choose it from the list.
   • To bookmark a specific page in the publication, select **A page in your publication** and select the target page number.

5. Click **OK** to confirm your choices.

To delete bookmarks and anchors:

1. Choose **Bookmark Manager...** from the Tools menu.

2. In the bookmark tree, select an entry for deletion, then click the **Remove** button. You'll be asked if you want to remove unused anchors.

OR

1. Click **Bookmark...** from the Insert menu (or **Insert Bookmark...** from the right-click menu).

2. In the Insert Bookmark dialog, click the **Delete Anchor** button.

3. From the dialog, you can either leave or delete all bookmarks or hyperlinks to the anchor independently of each other. Click **Yes** or **No** as appropriate.

Unlike hyperlinks, bookmarks also work as actual links within PagePlus publications. You can use the Bookmark Manager as a jumping-off point to any bookmarked entry.

Creating a PDF slideshow

The creation of PDF slideshows takes PagePlus's PDF publishing a step further. While a PDF file shows the exact replication of your original project for electronic distribution or printing, the PDF slideshow feature does the same, but with the intention of creating automated multimedia presentations. These can be shared by email and viewed without the need for special presentation software.

The main features of PDF slideshow include:

- Advance of each slide manually or automatically.

- Creation of multi-section slides from individual PagePlus pages.

- Use of slide-specific layer control (switch layers on or off).

- Freedom to reorder your slideshow.

- Apply slide-specific transition effects.

- Control of slide duration.

- Play a soundtrack for single slides or for the entire slideshow.

To publish a slideshow:

1. Select **Publish as PDF Slideshow...** from the File menu.

2. In the dialog, on the **General** tab, choose a default **Transition** type for all slides, e.g. Blinds, Wipe, or Dissolve. An individual slide can override this setting with its own transition setting.

3. Check **Manual Advance** if you don't want your slideshow to display slides one by one automatically—slides will be progressed manually by mouse-click or by pressing the space bar. For automatic slideshows, choose a **Duration**, i.e. the number of seconds each slide will remain on screen.

4. Uncheck **Preview PDF file in Acrobat** if you don't want to see a slideshow preview immediately after publishing.

5. When your slideshow reaches the last page you can **Loop slideshow** continuously or **Return to normal view** to exit the slideshow.

6. In the **Compatibility** field, select a version of Acrobat Reader. You'll get best results by using the latest version, but if your intended audience is unlikely to have the latest Reader software, you may opt for an earlier version.

7. For accompanying music, in the **Media** box, click the **Open** button to navigate to and select an audio file (WAV, MP3 and AIFF files supported).

8. For multi-section slides, from the **Slides** tab, duplicate or copy a selected slide with the **Insert** or **Copy** button, respectively. Delete a slide if needed, or rearrange the playback order of existing slides with the **Up** or **Down** buttons. For more information, see Multi-section slides (see p. 217).

9. The Compression, Security and Advanced tabs are as described in Exporting PDF files (see p. 213), and should be set accordingly. For most slideshows, the Compression tab's **Downsample Image** option should be checked and set to 96dpi (suitable for on-screen display).

10. Click **OK**. In the dialog, save your named PDF file to a chosen location. If **Preview PDF file in Acrobat** was checked, your slideshow will start to run automatically.

Multi-section slides

One strength of the slideshow feature comes from the ability to make 'multi-section' slide variants based on a single PagePlus page (this is done using page layers). Multi-section slides allow you to build up an image in sections; display multiple images and text objects sequentially on the same page; show and hide page elements; and so on. Simply create slides based on the original page then edit them by switching on/off specific layers to create unique slides. A few examples...

*   Create time-delayed bulleted lists—great for mouse- or pointer-driven presentations.

*   Introduce artistic elements to your page over time.

*   Change photos over time.

As you have full control over each slide's layers, you can design simple to complex designs based on which layer objects you choose to adopt. This, and the ability to assign different transition types and slide durations per slide, means that you have in-built flexibility when designing your slideshow. Your original PagePlus document needs to be designed with this in mind.

To create multi-section slides:

1. In the **Slides** tab of the **Publish PDF Slideshow** dialog, choose a page from which you want to create a slide and click the **Insert** or **Copy** button. The former inserts a chosen slide above the currently selected slide as a copy; the latter simply places a copy above a selected slide.

2. Select the new slide and click the **Properties** button.

3. Set a slide-specific **Transition** and **Duration** (in seconds) from the drop-down menus.

4. Uncheck any layers which you don't want to be part of the slide to make it distinct from other slides.

5. Click the ⊞ browse button and then browse to and select a **Media** file, which will play while the slide is displayed. For the slide's duration, this will override any default media file set up to play throughout your slideshow.

6. Repeat the insert, copy, and layer control for another slide, building up your multi-section slide arrangement.

> To undo the slide properties settings (reset the content of your slideshow so that there is only one slide per page), click the **Reset** button on the **Slides** tab.

Sharing by email

The widespread availability of the Internet means that colleagues, family and friends are now only a quick email away. Higher line speeds via Broadband connections open up new opportunities for sharing publications either as native PagePlus publications (.PPP) or as HTML. PagePlus will create an email from your standard email program (e.g., Outlook) either as a file attachment or within the body of your email, respectively.

Sharing PagePlus publications

1. With your publication open and in the currently active window, select **Send...** from the File menu.

   If the email program is not loaded, a Choose Profile dialog lets you select your email program, then a new email message is displayed with document attached. If already loaded, your email program automatically attaches your publication to a new email message.

2. Add the recipient's valid email address to the **To...** field (or equivalent).

3. Select the **Send** button (or equivalent) on your email program as for any other email message.

> An Internet connection is required for the emailing of pictures.

Interested in sharing content with recipients who may not be using PagePlus? The **Send page as HTML** feature lets you dispatch any page, safe in the knowledge that the email recipient(s) will be able to view your content exactly as intended (including all pictures and hyperlinks) because all referenced images are embedded locally with the message. This is a great method for publicising your publication (send your title page), providing work examples, email-ready photo albums or even datasheets.

> If you'd like to create blogs, birthday invites, holiday photo albums, or business emails you can save time by adopting an email-ready design template (click on **Use Design Template** in the Startup Wizard).

Sharing as HTML

1. With your publication open, select the page you would like to send.

2. Select **Send page as HTML...** from the File menu. The page is added to the body of a newly created HTML-based email message.

3. Add the recipient's valid email address to the **To...** field (or equivalent).

4. Select the **Send** button (or equivalent) on your email program.

> This method shares a single page only. To share a multi-page publication with recipients who don't use PagePlus, consider outputting your project as a PDF and then send the PDF as an attachment.

Using
PDF Forms

Getting started with PDF forms

The continuing development of Adobe's® Acrobat® technology means that great new possibilities are available to PagePlus. One of the most exciting is the use of electronic-based PDF forms—these allow information to be collected from readers of your publication in an efficient and modern manner. In much the same way as traditional paper forms are used to collect information (remember your last Tax Return!), PDF forms offer the same form completion concepts, but increase the interactivity between publisher and audience by using an electronic medium.

Some common form types include Application forms, Contact Information forms, Request forms, Feedback forms, and Guest books.

- One thing in common with all PDF forms is that they have to be published as PDF to operate. A PagePlus .PPP file with form functionality must be converted to PDF with **File>Publish as PDF**.

Form Structure

The building blocks of a form comprise a mixture of text, graphics and **Form fields**. Form fields collect recipient data and can be added, moved and modified in a similar way to more familiar objects in PagePlus such as graphics and table elements. A field can be a Text field, Radio Button, Combo box, List box, Check box or a simple button.

- From the form recipient's perspective, information is typed into text boxes or selected from check boxes, radio buttons, or drop-down boxes. The information entered can be numeric, textual, or a mixture of both. It is possible to arrange and lock form fields, plus control the order in which form fields can be navigated (see Designing your PDF forms in PagePlus Help).

- Each field has its own set of **Form Field Properties** relating to its appearance, its value(s), validation, calculations, and the action expected of the field.

In PagePlus, the form should be integrated into your Page design as you develop your publication. The form's functionality only then becomes active when a PDF of the form is generated. When a form recipient enters data into form fields the data can be collected as described below.

JavaScript is used to allow interactivity in your PDF forms. It drives formatting, validation, calculations, and actions—all key functions in PDF form development.

How is data collected?

Several methods exist for collecting forms once they have been completed.

(**1**) By Hardcopy **Print.**

(**2**) You can **Save Data to e-mail** (alternatively you can save data within the form).

(**3**) You can **Submit Data to Web** (a CGI application; by submission to a web-enabled server/database).

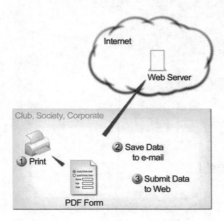

Creating PDF forms

Adding form fields

A series of form fields can be added to the page, depending on the type of form you want to create. Typically a mix of form fields will make up your finished form design.

Fields are created from the Form toolbar or via **Insert>Form Field**. You assign an internal unique name to each field and then set a variety of properties. Each form field has its own set of Form Field Properties which can be modified to suit your form implementation.

> The Form toolbar is turned off by default. Display it by going to **View>Toolbars>Form**.

Icon	Form Field Name	When to use?
ok	Button*	Use when specifying an action that can be triggered by a button click.
	Submit button*	Use when sending the form recipient's completed form data to Serif Web Resources or to your own Web server. A Form Submit Wizard is activated to enable quick and easy button setup.
	Reset button*	Use when you want to add a button to clear all form fields of data (often complements the above Submit button).
	Print button*	Use when you want to add a print button to your form.
✗	Check Box	Ideal when you want to multiply select a series of options displayed side by side. A good alternative to a Combo Box or List box if space allows.
I	Text Field	Use for adding text, numbers or a mixture of both.

	Combo Box	For selection from a scrollable list of items in a drop-down menu where only one item can be selected. The box also allows data entry to be input into this box type. Smaller than a List Box.
	List Box	For selection from a scrollable list of items; supports multiple selection and advanced actions on selection of menu items.
	Radio Button	Good for selection of a single mutually exclusive item from a grouped subset of choices.
	Signature	Used for the digital signing of secure documents. See PagePlus Help.

* This button shares a drop down menu with other buttons marked with an asterisk. The button type previously chosen will always be display on the Form toolbar.

To add a form field:

1. Select one of the form field buttons on the **Form** toolbar.

2. Move your ⊞ cursor to the location at which you want to place your form field and click once.

3. Right-click on the form field and choose **Form Field Properties** from the drop-down menu.

4. In the **General** tab, overwrite the current **Name** with a unique internal name. You can also choose several other optional settings (see General tab).

5. Go to the **Options** tab. Depending on the file type, use this to enter list items, change the style, change the caption name and set defaults and other options.

6. (Optional) Go to the **Actions** tab and click the **Add** button.

7. (Optional) In the resulting Action dialog, select an Event that will be used to trigger the action.

8. (Optional) Choose an **Action** from the drop-down menu.

9. (Optional) Change the properties displayed under the selected action. The options shown change depending to the action selected.

Form field properties

Form field properties control how the form field will operate when the form recipient enters their input. A series of tabs are arranged so that some tabs, e.g. **General**, **Appearance**, **Options**, or **Actions**, are common to all the form fields but others, such as **Format**, **Validation** and **Calculations** are only displayed for text fields and combo boxes.

To access Form Field Properties:

1. To view the properties do one of the following:

   - Right-click on a selected form field and choose **Form Field Properties**.

   - Double-click the form field.

   - Select the form field, and click the [button] button from the **Form** toolbar.

2. Click on one of several tabs for editing: General, Appearance, Options, Actions, Validate, or Calculate.

3. Click the **OK** or **Cancel** button to exit the dialog.

Publishing your PDF Form

Once your PDF form is completed you can publish the form using **File>Publish as PDF**. See Exporting PDF files on p. 213 for more information.

> If you Publish as PDF using PDF/X-1 or PDF/X-1a compatibility, any PDF form fields present will be converted to graphics and will not be available. Choose an Acrobat option instead.

Collecting data from forms

Via Hardcopy Printout

This is a simple fill-in and print to hardcopy solution. This is great if your form recipients are located together, perhaps in the same office.

> ☞ If using Acrobat® Reader®, any completed form data will be lost when you close your completed PDF form. Exceptions exist when using Standard or Professional software.

Within the PDF File

Alternatively, it is possible to store form data within the PDF Form itself by using the **Save** or **Save As...** command. One condition of this is that the form recipient must be using one of the following versions of Acrobat software:

* Adobe® Acrobat® 6.0 (or later) Standard or Professional.

* Adobe® Acrobat® 7.0 (or later) Elements.

> ☞ Acrobat® Reader® software (6.0 and above) is unable to save form data within the form. However, for form recipients with Acrobat® Reader® 7.0 software, **Reader Extensions** software is available from http://www.adobe.com/products/livecycle/readerextensions/ which will permit form data to be saved locally with the form. This is called rights-based PDF Form handling.

Using email

If you can save data within the PDF form then it's clear that you can email the completed form to the form originator. With the completed form still open, use **File>E-mail** to send the email to the intended recipient.

Via the Web

* Your PDF Form can be configured to be Web ready by passing completed form data to a CGI application on a Web server. This would typically be a server-sided web page designed to process the data and pass it to either a text file, database or other storage location. As an example, new subscriber details, collected via a PDF Form, can be sent automatically to a previously configured "subscribers" database.

- All Web-ready forms have one thing in common—they must be submitted to allow data to be collected. Typically, you may have come across this on web sites when you enter details into a form then submit the data by pressing a Submit button. The same applies for PDF forms—a **Submit** button can be configured in order to submit the form data to the Web server. You can either create the button unaided or use the **Form Submit Wizard** (see below). Either way, the use of the submit process is the major difference between web-ready and other less dynamic forms.

- The Web process, as mentioned, requires a Web server to operate. Not everyone will have access to or even want to operate their own Web server so, as an alternative to this, you can use **Serif Web Resources**. This is a free Web to email gateway service which will collect your valued form data at Serif and send it to your email address—the service does require that you firstly have a Customer login (for security reasons), which will allow you to create, edit and delete Form IDs via a web page accessible from the Wizard. The Form ID, a unique 30-digit number, is required for the service to operate and is generated automatically when you enter your destination email address in the above web page.

> No personal data will be stored on Serif Web servers. All form data is redirected in real time.

Submitting Form Data

- The submission of form data sounds a very complicated operation but by using a Form Submit Wizard the process is relatively straightforward. The Wizard not only creates a Submit button for your form, but configures the underlying submit process and the format in which your form data is to be stored in.

- The submit process is made either to Serif Web Resources or to your own Web server address (e.g., http://testserver.global.com/forms/collect.asp).

- Form data can be stored in several data formats:

Data Format	via Serif Web Resources	To Web Server
HTML	ASCII. The form data can be read directly in your email without acrobat software.	ASCII. Use for sending form data directly to the Server-sided Databases, as in Web forms.
FDF	The form data is emailed as an attachment, and when opened, is reunited with the original form to allow data to be read In Situ.	binary. The form data can be stored on the web server.
XFDF	As for FDF but with additional XML-based support.	binary. The form data can be stored on the web server.
PDF	Not available.	binary. The form data can be stored on the web server. Useful for preserving digital signatures.

To run the Form Submit Wizard:

1. Select the [⬚] **Submit** button from the Button flyout menu on the **Form** toolbar.

2. In the first step, start the wizard by clicking the Next> button.

3. Choose either Serif Web Resources or your own server as the destination of your form recipient's data. The former is appropriate if you don't have access to your own web server. Depending on your choice, you can:

   1. **For Serif Web Resources**, click **Next>**.

   2. Click the **Get a Form ID** button to display Serif's customer login web page. This page is where you log onto your customer account to enter firstly your email address to send form data to, and secondly to generate a unique Form ID for use in the secure email communication.

3. At the web page, if you already have a customer login you can enter your email address and password. For new customer you must register before continuing.

4. After login, select the **add form** link to enter the email address that you want your form data to be sent to.

5. Click the **Add Form** button. This generates an entry in the displayed list from which a 30-digit Form ID can be copied.

6. Paste the Form ID directly from the web page into the input field in your Wizard dialog.

7. Click the **Next>** button.

8. Select a Data format from the drop-down menu that you would like to store and transport your form data. Select one of: HTML, FDF, or XFDF (see above).

OR

1. **For your own Web server**, click **Next>**.

2. Add your Web Server address to the displayed field, click **Next>**. NOTE: this should not be a file directory but a valid Web site on the Intranet/Internet.

3. Choose a data format for exporting the form data. Select one of: HTML, FDF, PDF or XFDF (see above). NOTE: You must ensure that your server is able to process the above data formats.

4. Finish the Wizard process by clicking the **Finish** button.

5. Move your ⊞ cursor to the location for your button and click once.

> The Submit button settings can be edited (as for other form fields) by right-clicking and selection of Form Field Properties. This will allow form fields to be included/excluded from data collection.

Producing
Web Pages

Getting started in Web mode

How easy is it to create your own Web site with PagePlus? It can be as simple as selecting a preset design template and editing the headings and accompanying text. And no matter how much customizing you choose to do after that, the whole job won't be nearly as complicated as developing your own site from first principles. So, if you're already comfortable using PagePlus for paper publications, you'll find it easy going. If you're just beginning, you'll learn to use PagePlus tools as you go.

Essentially, PagePlus takes the pages you've laid out and converts them to HTML. In fact, the Web design templates simplify things further by providing you with a variety of starter layouts, professionally designed expressly for Web display.

Starting a new Web publication

Paper Publishing mode is the familiar PagePlus environment for creating print publications. However, before developing your web site PagePlus must operate in **Web Publishing mode**. The Web Publishing mode includes special features, such as menu items and custom settings, to facilitate creation of Web pages.

> If you choose any of the Web Page design templates after starting PagePlus you will be in Web Publishing mode automatically.

Anyone using Web Publishing mode for the first time should begin by creating a simple Web site using a design template. You'll find a selection of templates available by default, plus lots more on the PagePlus X3 Resource DVD. (For more details about the Resource DVD, contact Serif.)

To create a new Web publication using a Design Template:

1. Launch PagePlus or choose **New>New from Startup Wizard** from the File menu.

2. In the Startup Wizard, select the **Use Design Template** option, select the **Web Publishing** category on the left, and examine the samples on the right. Click the sample that's closest to the site you want to create, then click **Open**.

Just as in Paper Publishing mode, you also have the option of starting a new publication from scratch, or opening an existing publication.

If you'd like to build on previous work you've done with PagePlus, you can also take an existing paper publication and convert it to a Web publication.

To turn an existing PagePlus (paper) publication into a Web site:

- Open the publication in Paper Publishing mode and choose **Switch to Web Publishing** from the File menu.

To adjust size/orientation of the current publication:

1. Choose **Page Setup...** from the File menu.
2. Set page dimensions as **Standard** for VGA monitors (recommended), **Wide** for SVGA, or **Custom**. For a custom setting, enter page dimensions in pixels.

Viewing hyperlinks in your publication

The **Hyperlink Manager** gives you an overview of all the hyperlinks in your publication or Web site.

To display the Hyperlink Manager:

- Choose **Hyperlink Manager...** from the Tools menu.

The Hyperlink Manager dialog displays both object and text hyperlinks in your publication, listed by page number. The entries are in "from/to" format, showing each link's source object type and its destination page or URL.

To display a hyperlink for closer inspection:

- Click to select the link entry and click the **Display** button.

To remove or modify a hyperlink:

- Click to select the link entry and click the **Remove** or **Modify** button. To modify the hyperlink, select a new link destination type and/or target.

Adding hotspots

A hotspot is a transparent hyperlink region on a Web page. Usually placed on top of images, hotspots act like "buttons" that respond when clicked in a Web browser. They are especially useful if you want the visitor to be able to click on different parts of a picture (such as a graphic "menu" or map of your site).

To define a hotspot:

1. On the Insert menu, choose **Web Object**, and then click **Hotspot**.

2. Click and drag to draw a rectangular hotspot region. The **Hyperlinks** dialog opens.

3. Click to select the link destination type, and enter the specific hyperlink target—an Internet page, a page on your Web site, an email address, local file, or an object's anchor.

4. Click **OK**.

To modify a hotspot hyperlink:

- Using the **Pointer Tool**, double-click the hotspot.
  OR

  Click to select the hotspot, then click the  **Hyperlink** button on the Standard toolbar.

The **Hyperlinks** dialog opens with the current hotspot link target shown.

- To modify the hyperlink, select a new link destination type and/or target.

- To remove the hyperlink, click the **Remove** button.

Editing hotspots

You can move and resize hotspots on the page, just like other objects. A selected hotspot has both an outer bounding box and an inner outline.

To move or resize a hotspot:

- Click to select the hotspot.

- To move, drag from the centre, or from the hotspot's bounding box. To constrain the hotspot to vertical or horizontal movement, hold down the **Shift** key while dragging.

- To resize, drag on its outer (bounding box) handles.

By editing the inner outline, you can convert rectangular hotspots into freeform shapes that closely match the parts of the underlying graphic you want to be "hot." To edit the outline, first move the mouse pointer over the hotspot's inner outline until the cursor changes to indicate whether you're over a node or a line.

Web site colours

A Web site may have an adopted colour scheme, selected by using the **Schemes** tab. Each scheme has a name and consists of five complementary basic colours (plus additional Web colours) which you can apply to any design element (see Using schemes on p. 193).

A selection of schemes (named "WWW 1" through "WWW 9") appearing at the bottom of the tab's scheme list are specifically designed for Web use.

The currently set colour scheme is also shown at the bottom of the Swatches tab for convenience. For example for the colour scheme "WWW3", numbers or letters represent basic or Web colour sets, respectively:

Web colours

Web sites have several special **Web colour** settings, usually defined as part of a colour scheme in the **Scheme Manager** (for details, see Using schemes on p. 193). You'll need to know about these settings, even if you haven't applied scheme colours to other elements in your site.

- The **Hyperlink** colour (labelled **H** above) applies to hyperlinked text **before** it's been clicked on.

- The **Followed Hyperlink** colour (labelled **F**), applies to hyperlinked text after a visitor has clicked to "follow" the link.

- The **Active Hyperlink** colour (labelled **A**), applies to hyperlinked text when a visitor's mouse button is depressed. Typically this is the colour shown after clicking and before the hyperlink's page is displayed.

- The **Rollover** colour (labelled **R**), applies to hyperlinked text when a visitor's mouse button rolls over it.

- A Web site's **Background** is a solid colour with the option of overlaying a tiled (repeated) picture, usually a bitmap pattern. The tiled picture option works just like desktop "wallpaper," so a small bitmap can go a long way. The background will fill any blank space left in the browser when displayed on a larger screen.

  If you use a picture background with transparent regions, the Background colour is still active and will show through; otherwise the picture will cover the background colour.

- The **On-page** colour allows you to have a distinct colour for the defined page area. If set to transparent, it will display the current background colour.

The easiest way to apply new Web colours is to select a different colour scheme by clicking a sample on the **Schemes** tab.

You can also change any of the Web colours within a scheme using the Scheme Manager, in the same way that you would modify the scheme's five basic colours. See Using schemes on p. 193.

Setting custom page backgrounds

The Web colours defined in the Scheme Manager normally apply throughout the site, but you can override the Scheme Manager's Background picture/colour setting for any particular page.

To set a custom page background:

1. Choose **Web Site Properties...** from the File menu.

2. On the **Background** tab, uncheck **Use Scheme Manager settings** and set new options for **Background colour** and/or **Use picture** and/or **On-page colour.**

> The settings apply only to the current page.

Setting Web picture display options

When you export a publication as a Web site, PagePlus applies certain global settings to determine how each image—whether drawn, pasted in, or imported—ends up as a separate bitmap displayed on the Web page.

The following conversion settings are used for Web publishing:

- Each image in the publication is exported as a separate file.

- Any image you inserted is exported as the original file, using its original file name.

- Inserted metafiles and all other graphics are converted to JPEG images, using a compression quality setting of 10 (low compression, high detail). For these images, PagePlus automatically generates file names, using incremental numbering (IMG1, IMG2, etc.) that continues each time you export.

Global export options and setting export formats are described in more detail in the PagePlus Help.

Choosing Web page properties

There's more to creating a successful Web site than designing the pages. It's a good idea to browse the **Site Properties** dialog, accessible from **File>Web Site Properties** and review a variety of settings you might not otherwise have considered!

Site Properties/Page tab

Some of the options on the dialog's **Page** tab pertain just to the current page, while others apply to the site as a whole. The Web page **title**, which will appear in the title bar of the visitor's Web browser, can serve to unify the pages and focus the site's identity, as well as aid navigation. Each page in your site can have its own title, but you may prefer to use the same title on multiple pages (in effect, a site title). An easy way to do this is to start with a blank page, give it a title, then replicate that page. Copies of that page will have the same title.

Each page also has a **file name** when it's published. You can specify file names individually; otherwise PagePlus automatically generates them.

Check the instructions from your Web service provider as to their naming conventions for Home Pages and file extensions. By default, PagePlus names your first (Home) page index.html—the standard file name a browser will be looking for. Depending on the particular server in use, however, some other name may be required. Likewise, the extension .htm is sometimes used for pages.

Adding animation effects

PagePlus lets you add two varieties of eye-catching animation effects to any Web page: **animated marquees** and **GIF animations**. Either way, you can preview the animation and/or customize the effect. Once placed into your Web publication, the animations appear static, but they will spring to life once the site has been exported and a visitor views your page in a Web browser.

Adding sound and video

PagePlus lets you augment your Web pages with sound and video files in a variety of standard formats, including both **non-streaming** and **streaming** media.

(Non-streaming files must download in entirety to a user's computer before they begin playing; streaming files require a special player that buffers incoming data and can start playing before the whole clip has arrived.)

There are actually two sound playback options—**background sound**, where a sound loads and plays automatically when a specific page is first displayed in the visitor's Web browser, and **linked sound**, triggered by a mouse click (for example on an icon or hyperlinked object). The supported audio formats are .wav, .mp3, Aiff (.aiff, .aif, .aifc), .au, MIDI (.mid, .midi), and RealAudio (.ra, .ram).

Linked video works like linked sound. Supported video formats are .avi, QuickTime (.mov, .qt), MPEG (.mpg, .mpeg, .mpe, .mpv), and RealVideo (.ram, .rv).

To add background sound to a page:

1. Choose **Web Site Properties...** from the File menu and select the **Page** tab.

2. Browse to the sound file you want to add, or enter its path name directly.

3. If you do *not* wish to embed the file in your publication, uncheck the "Embed" option.
   Note: If you choose not to embed your source files, we suggest you keep them together in a subfolder named "Media" or the like. When you publish your site, PagePlus exports and copies both embedded and non-embedded files into a common folder.

4. To have the sound play back as a continuous loop, check "Loop sound". Otherwise, it will play just once.

The sound file will download and play back when the Web page displays in a browser.

With both linked sound and linked video, the basic question is how you want the visitor to be able to trigger the playback of a given media file. PagePlus offers the same basic options for both kinds of media:

- **From a hyperlinked object or hotspot:** You start with an existing object in the publication, and hyperlink it to the media file, or use a hotspot over an image.

- **From a picture:** You select an external picture file, which PagePlus then imports and links to the media file.

- **From an icon:** PagePlus provides an icon pre-linked to the media file. You then position the icon on your page.

- **Inline:** A media "player" will be visible on your published Web page (rather than appearing after the user clicks a link, icon, or picture). In PagePlus, you'll see a marker on the page where the player will appear.

With the first option, the media file remains external and can't be embedded in your publication. The last two options give you the choice of embedding the media file.

To add linked sound or video to a page:

1. To link from an icon, picture, or inline player (options 2 to 4), choose **Web Object...** from the Insert menu and select either **Sound...** or **Video...** from the submenu.

2. Browse to locate the media file name.

3. Select a link display option.

4. If you do *not* wish to embed the file in your publication, uncheck the "Embed" option.
   Note: If you choose not to embed your source files, we suggest you keep them together in a single subfolder, named "Media" or the like. When you publish your site, PagePlus exports and copies both embedded and non-embedded files into a common folder.

5. Click **OK** to close the dialog, then click (or click and drag) with the cursor to place the icon, picture, or marker on your page.

Adding Java applets

Java is a cross-platform, object-oriented programming language used to create mini-applications called **applets** that can be attached to Web pages and that run when the page is viewed in a Web browser. PagePlus lets you add Java applets to your Web publications. You don't have to write your own! Plenty of applets are available online—for example animation, interface components, live information updating, two-way interaction, and many more.

Consult PagePlus help to find out more about adding Java applets to your web pages.

Publishing a Web site to a local folder

Even though you may have saved your Web site as a PagePlus publication, it's not truly a "Web site" until you've converted it to HTML and image files—in other words, a format that can be viewed in a Web browser. In PagePlus, this conversion process is called publishing the site. You can publish the site either to a local folder (on a hard disk) or to the Web itself. To review the basics, see Getting started in Web mode on p. 235.

Publishing the site to a local folder lets you preview the pages in your own browser prior to publishing them on the Web. You may find it convenient to keep your browser program open, and go back and forth between PagePlus and the browser. This way you can make changes to a single page in PagePlus, publish just the one page, then switch to your browser and preview that page to make sure everything appears just as you want it.

To publish the site to a local folder:

1. Choose **Web Site Properties...** from the File menu and double-check export settings, particularly those on the Graphics tab.

2. Choose **Publish Site** from the File menu and select **to Disk Folder...** from the submenu.

3. In the dialog, locate the folder where you wish to store the output files by clicking the **Choose Folder...** button. You can create a new folder under any selected folder with the **Make New Folder** button. Click **OK**.

4. Either check the **Publish All Pages** option, or in the site structure tree, check which specific page(s) to publish. This can save a lot of time by skipping the export of pages you haven't changed.

5. Click **OK**.

After PagePlus has finished exporting the selected pages, you'll be asked if you want to launch your Web Browser to view your pages. Click **Yes** if you wish to do this.

Previewing your Web site in a browser

Previewing your site in a Web browser is an essential step before publishing it to the Web. It's the only way you can see just how your PagePlus publication will appear to a visitor. Bear in mind that pages generally load much more quickly from a hard disk than they will over the Web. If performance is sluggish from a hard disk, it's time to subtract some graphics, divide the content into more (and smaller) pages, or run the Layout Checker again.

To preview your Web site from a local hard disk:

- Choose **Publish Site** from the File menu and select **to Disk Folder...** from the submenu. After publishing the site (or selected pages), answer **Yes** when asked if you want to run a Web browser to preview your pages.
  OR

- Choose **Preview in Browser>** from the File menu, then choose a **Preview Page in <browser name>...** or **Preview Site in <browser name>...** to use an external browser. The <browser name> will reflect which browsers are currently installed, e.g. the entry may read "Preview Page in Internet Explorer." If you have more than one browser installed, you can select which browser(s) to display on the submenu. The page or site is exported to a temporary folder and appears in the specified browser.
  OR

- (if you've previously published the site to a folder) Open your Web browser and use its Open File command to display a page from the site, usually the index.html (Home Page) file.

Publishing to the Web

Publishing to the Web involves a few more steps, but is basically as simple as publishing to a local folder! You can specify that all Web pages are published or only pages updated since your last "publish."

To publish your site to the Web:

1. On the File menu, choose **Web Site Properties...** and verify your export settings, particularly those on the **Graphics** tab.

2. On the File menu, choose **Publish Site** and then select **to Web....**

If this is your first time publishing to the Web, the **Account Details** dialog opens (with no account information present). You'll need to set up at least one account before you can proceed.

3. In the dialog, enter the following:

   - The **Account name** can be any name of your choice. You'll use it to identify this account in PagePlus (in case you have more than one).

   - The **FTP address** of your Web host will be a specific URL as supplied by your Internet service provider (ISP).

   - Unless directed by your provider, leave the **Port number** set at "21."

   - Leave the **Folder** box blank unless directed by your provider, or if you want to publish to a specific subfolder of your root directory.

- You'll also need a **Username** and **Password**. These are pre-assigned by your provider and will most likely correspond to email login settings. Enter the password exactly as given to you, using correct upper- and lower-case spelling, or the host server may not recognize it. If you don't want to re-enter your password with each upload, check **Save password** to record the password on your computer.

- **Passive mode**: Leave checked unless you have FTP connection problems (check with your ISP). ISPs can operate passive or active FTP modes of operation.

- **Web site URL**: Set your site's URL. This allows you to view your site from a dialog after any FTP upload.

- Click **OK** to close the **Account Details** dialog.

You can also use the dialog to **Add** another account, and **Copy**, **Edit**, or **Delete** an account selected from the drop-down menu. It's a good idea to test your new or modified account by clicking the **Test** button—if the account details are valid, a dialog indicating successful connection displays.

4. If you've set up at least one account, the **Manage FTP Accounts** dialog opens. In the dialog, the last used account name is shown in the drop-down menu; its settings are displayed in subsequent boxes. You can use the drop-down menu to switch to another account, if you have set up more than one.

5. Click the **Upload...** button. PagePlus seeks an Internet connection, then:

- If uploading for the first time, selected files will be uploaded directly. OR

- If uploading to an existing site (must be created with PagePlus), an **Uploading Files** dialog is displayed showing local file action (whether files will be added (Add), will replace the live files (Replace), or will not be updated (Leave)).

  In the dialog, select either the **Incremental Update** or **Full upload** button. Choose the former to upload only files that have altered since the last upload. You'll see a message when all files have been successfully copied. Click **OK**.

Gathering server information

If you have an email account, your contract with the email service provider may allow you a certain amount of file space (e.g., 25MB) on their server where you can store files, including the files that comprise a Web site. Or you may have a separate "Web space" arrangement with a specialized Internet service provider. It's up to you to establish an account you can use for Web publishing.

Maintaining your Web site

Once you've published your site to the Web, you'll need to maintain the pages on your site by updating content periodically: adding or changing text, pictures, and links, also file/folder deletion or renaming. Making the content changes is easy enough—all the originals are right there in your publication!

To maintain files and folders on your Web site:

1. Choose **Publish Site** from the File menu and select **Maintain Web Site...** from the submenu. The Account Details dialog appears.
2. Select your FTP account name (from the drop-down menu), your Username and Password. Type the correct path in the Folder box, if required by your provider.
3. Click **Maintain**.

PagePlus seeks an Internet connection and displays a dialog showing the navigable web site's folders in a left-hand window and any selected folder's contents in the adjacent window.

4. Use standard Windows Explorer conventions to perform maintenance tasks:
   • Click on the column headers to change the current sort, or drag to change the column width.
   • The top row of buttons lets you view up one level, create a new folder, delete a selected item, upload/download a file, and refresh the window.
   • Right-click to **Open**, **Download**, **Delete**, or **Rename** any file or folder.
   • You can **Ctrl**-click to select multiple files or **Shift**-click to select a range of files.
   • To move one or more selected files, drag them into the destination folder.
   • To delete the entire web site, click the **View** button next to your selected Serif Manifest file—in the dialog, click the **Delete all managed files** button.

   Remember to use the lower information window which displays a running log of each maintenance task and its status.

5. When you're done, click the window's  **Close** button to terminate the FTP connection and return to PagePlus.

Index

2D, 172
  filter effects, 172
3D, 175
  filter effects, 175
  Instant 3D, 179
3D Lighting, 175, 178
3D Reflection Map, 177
Adobe Acrobat (PDF files), 22,
    213, 214, 216
  bookmark lists in, 214
  exporting, 213
  importing, 22
albums (photo), 153
alignment, 61, 97
  of objects, 61
  of paragraphs, 97
anchors
  hyperlinking to, 70
animation effects
  adding to Web page, 241
animation effects (Web), 241
arrows, 170
artistic text, 85
  on a path, 90
Artistic Text Tool, 86
AutoCorrect, 118
AutoFit, 82
  of frame text, 82
  of path text, 92
  to table row/column cell
      contents, 126
AutoFlow, 83, 155
  of frame text, 83
  of images, 155
AutoSpell, 119
AVI (Web multimedia), 242
background (master page), 31
background colour or scheme of
    Web pages, 239
banners, 20, 29
  printing, 205
Bézier curves, 165
bitmap fills, 191

bitmap transparency, 199
bitmaps, 147
  importing (see also images), 147
  replacing, 152
bleed area guides, 42
Blur effect, 173
BMP images, 147
booklets, 20, 29
  printing, 205
bookmarks, 214
  for PDF files, 214
BookPlus, 137
books, 137
borders, 69
boxes, 170
bulleted lists, 106, 111
Bump Map effects, 176
Calendar Event Manager, 130
Calendar Wizard, 130
calendars, 130
  events for, 132
  public holidays for, 132
calligraphic lines, 167
cap setting (lines), 168
chapters (books), 137
character styles, 104
characters
  symbols, 115
circle, 170
Clear formatting, 98, 107
Clipboard, 56
  copying and pasting to or from,
      56
closing PagePlus, 24
CMYK palette, 196
colour, 189
  applying fill colours, 189, 190
  creating your own colours, 196
  in Web publications, 238
  palettes, 190, 196
  schemes, 193, 238
Colour Fill effect, 172
Colour Picker, 196

Colour Selector, 198
Colour tab, 167, 189
column
    and row guides, 43
    blinds, 79
    margins, 79
Combine Curves, 65
commercial printing, 207
conical fills, 191
conical transparency, 199
connection points, 184
    editing, 186
Connector Tool, 184
connectors, 184
    editing, 186
constraining movement of objects,
    59
Context toolbar
    curve, 166
    frame, 80
    mesh warp, 178
    shadow, 174
    text, 97
converting an object to an image,
    62
correction lists, 118
Crop to Shape, 67
Crop tools, 65
cropping objects, 65
Curve context toolbar, 166
curves. See lines
custom publication setup, 29
dashed lines, 167
data sources (for mail merge), 141
databases, 133
    inserting (into tables), 133
date and time fields, 116
Default paragraph font, 105
default properties, 24
deforming (Mesh Warp), 178
design templates, 20
dictionary, 119
    personal (spell-checking), 120
digital cameras, 158
dimensionality (Instant 3D), 179

dimensions (page), 29
distributing objects, 61
document information, 117
dot grid, 47
    snapping to, 55
double lines, 167
draw-type images
    importing, 147
Drop Cap, 106
Drop Shadow effect, 172
duplex printing (manual), 208
edges (border), 69
editing text, 92, 97
effects, 172, 175
    2D filter, 172
    3D filter, 175
    Instant 3D, 179
    Reflection Map, 177
Elbow Connector Tool, 184
elliptical fills, 191
elliptical transparency, 199
email
    sharing publications as HTML
        by, 219
    sharing publications by, 218
embedding vs. linking, 142, 149
Emboss effect, 172
endnotes, 97
envelope (mesh warp), 178
events (calendar), 132
exporting, 62, 213
    as PDF, 213
    objects as a picture, 62
extracting images, 160
facing pages, 29
Feather effect, 172
features (new), 3
fill and line properties, 163, 167,
    189, 190
Fill Tool, 191
fills, 189, 190
    Bitmap, 190
    gradient, 190
    solid, 189
filter effects, 172, 175

Find & Replace, 96
Fit Text to Curve, 91
flipping objects, 65
folded publications, 20, 29
    printing, 205
FontManager, 101, 104
fonts
    assigning, 99
    checking, 143
    dynamic installation of, 104
    FontManager, 104
    listing in publication, 143
    previewing, 99
    replace common, 99
    setting, 98
    substituting, 100
Fonts tab, 98
footers, 48
footnotes, 97
formatting
    clear text, 98
formatting numbers (tables), 129
formulas (tables), 129
frame effect (border), 69
frame margins, 76
frame text, 76
    defined (see also text frames),
        75
frames, 75
    applying fill colours, 189, 191
    applying transparency, 200
    for pictures, 147
    linking, 83
    picture, 150
    setup and layout, 79
functions (tables), 130
Gallery tab, 156
Gaussian Blur effect, 172
GIF animations (Web), 241
gradient colour fills, 190
    applying, 191
    editing, 193
gradient transparency, 199
grammar, 120

checking with Proof Reader,
    120
grid (dot), 47
groups, 56
    creating, 56
    resizing, 60
    ungrouping, 56
guides, 42
    for page margins, rows,
        columns, and bleeds, 42
    ruler, 46
    snapping to, 55
    sticky, 44
headers and footers, 48
holidays (public), 132
hotspots (Web), 236
HTML
    sending documents via email as,
        219
Hyperlink Manager, 236
hyperlinks
    adding, 70
    setting colour of, 239
    using Hyperlink Manager, 236
Image Cutout Studio, 160
images. See pictures
importing
    database tables, 133
    delimited files (for mail merge),
        141
    PagePlus documents, 22
    paint- and draw-type images,
        147
    PDF files, 22
    pictures, 147
    text, 75
    TWAIN images, 158
imposition
    of folded publications, 205
Increase level, 106, 113
indents, 44, 94
index, 136
    creating, 140
Inner Bevel effect, 172
Inner Glow effect, 172

Inner Shadow effect, 172
installation, 11
Instant 3D, 179
interface
  rulers, 44
  setting units, 45
  view options, 32
Internet Service Provider (ISP),
  245
Java applets (for Web), 243
Join setting (lines), 168
JPGs, 147, 240
  for Web, 240
  importing, 147
layers, 36
  adding, 38
  assigning master pages to, 36
  deleting, 38
  viewing, 35
layout guides, 42, 46, 55
  creating, 46
  setting, 42
  snapping to, 55
layout tools, 42, 44, 55
  dot grid, 47
  guides, 43
  rulers, 44
  snapping, 55
lighting, 175, 178
  3D Effect, 175, 178
line and fill properties, 163, 167,
  169, 189, 190
linear fills, 191
linear transparency, 199
lines, 164
  closing (to make shapes), 171
  combining, 68
  dashed, 167
  double, 167
  fitting text to, 91
  resizing, 59
  setting properties, 167
linking text frames, 83
linking vs. embedding, 142, 149
lists, 111

bulleted, 111
  multi-level, 113
  numbered, 111
locking object size or position, 60
logos, 87
LogoStudio, 87
mail and photo merge, 141
maintaining Web sites, 247
margin guides, 43
margins, 42
  mirrored, 43
  setting, 42
marquees, 241
  animated, adding to Web page,
    241
master pages, 36
  adding and removing, 36
  and layers, 40
  assigning, 36
  headers and footers on, 48
  overview, 31
  page numbers on, 48
  viewing and editing, 34
measuring objects, 44
Media Bar, 152
Mesh Warp, 178
metafiles, 62, 147
  exporting, 62
  importing, 147
  Serif, 62
mirrored margins, 43
Motion Blur effect, 172
MPEG (Web multimedia), 242
multi-level lists, 113
multilingual spell-checking, 119
multimedia, 242
multimedia (Web), 242
Multi-page view, 33
multiple open documents, 23
multiple pages, 204
  print preview, 204
  printing, 206
  viewing, 33
multiple selections, 54
named styles, 105

navigation, 34
new features in PagePlus X3, 3
Normal style, 105
Normal view, 33
numbered lists, 111
Object Style Manager, 182
object styles, 181
    saving, 183
objects
    aligning, 61
    applying mesh warp to, 178
    applying schemes to, 195
    converting, to pictures, 62
    copying, pasting, and
        duplicating, 56
    cropping, 65
    distributing, 61
    flipping, 65
    locking size or position, 60
    measuring, 44
    moving, 59
    ordering, 60
    pasting formatting of, 58
    replicating, 57
    resizing, 59
    reusing in different publications,
        156
    rotating, 64
    selecting individual, 53
    selecting more than one, 54
    setting default properties, 25
    snapping to dot grid or guides,
        55
opening an existing publication, 21
ordering objects, 60
Outer Bevel effect, 172
Outer Glow effect, 172
Outline effect, 172, 173
oval, 170
Page Manager, 35
Page Setup, 29
page size and orientation, 29
pages, 34, 35, 48
    adding, removing, and
        rearranging, 35

    numbering, 48, 138
    viewing, 32, 34
Pages tab, 34, 35
paint-type images, 147
    importing, 147
Palette
    Publication, 196
Palette Manager, 197, 198
palettes (colour), 139, 190, 196
paragraphs, 97
    alignment, 97
    setting indents for, 94
    setting tab stops for, 95
    styles, 104
Paste Format, 58
Paste Format Plus, 58
pasteboard area, 32
path text, 90
Pattern Map effects, 177
PDF files, 214
    adding bookmarks, 214
    importing, 22
    publishing, 140, 207, 213
    substituting fonts in, 23
PDF forms, 223
    collecting data from, 228
    creating, 225
PDF slideshows, 216
    multi-section, 217
Pen Tool, 164
Pencil Tool, 164
photos. See pictures
pictures, 69, 150
    adding via Media Bar to page,
        155
    borders for, 69
    colourizing, 189
    converting objects to, 62
    default sizes, 59
    deforming (Mesh Warp), 178
    exporting objects as, 62
    extracting parts of, 160
    for Web (overview), 240
    frames for, 150
    importing, 147

listing imported images in
  publication, 142
Media Bar for, 152
resizing, 59
wrapping text around, 110
Pillow Emboss effect, 172
PNGs, 147
  importing, 147
point size, 97
polygon, 170
posters, 20, 29
  printing, 205
PostScript output, 207
prepress options, 207
previewing, 204, 244
  the printed page, 204
  Web sites in Web browser, 244
printing, 203
  books, 140
  manual duplex, 208
  multiple pages, 206
  of banners, posters, booklets,
    and thumbnails, 205
  PDF files, 140
  previewing the page, 204
  professional, 207
  saving print profiles, 209
professional printing, 207
profiles, 19, 209
  saving print, 209
  workspace, 19
proofing tools
  previewing the printed page,
    204
  Proof Reader, 120
  Resource Manager, 142
  Spell Checker, 119
  Thesaurus, 121
public holidays (calendar), 132
Publication Palette, 196
  adding custom colours to, 196
  saving, 198
publications, 20
  copying to another computer,
    142

creating hyperlinks in, 70
creating, from design templates,
  20
for Web, 235
layers in, 31
layout guides, 43
master pages, 31
opening existing, 21
producing books, 137
saving, 24
setting dimensions, 29
sharing by email, 218
starting from scratch, 20
viewing hyperlinks in, 236
working with more than one, 23
publishing PDF files, 140, 213
publishing Web sites
  to local folder, 244
  to Web, 245
QuickClear and QuickFill (tables),
  128
QuickShape Tool, 170
QuickTime (Web multimedia), 242
Radial Blur effect, 172
raster images, 147
  importing, 147
readability, 120
  checking with Proof Reader,
    120
RealAudio/Video (Web), 242
reapply styles, 108
Reflection effect, 172
registration, 10
Resource Manager, 142
resources, 142
  listing imported resources in
    publication, 142
reverting to saved version, 21
RGB palette, 196
Rotate Tool, 64
row and column guides, 43
rulers, 44, 62
  setting units for, 45
saving a publication, 24
scaling (printing), 206

scanned images, 158
schemes, 193, 238
    colour, 193, 238
SDB (Serif Database) files, 141
selecting, 53, 92
    objects, 53
    text, 92
Serif MetaFile Format (SMF), 62,
    147
Serif Web Resources, 229
service provider (server)
    information, 246
SFM (Serif Font Map) files, 103
Shade/Tint slider, 190
shapes, 169
    applying transparency, 200
    changing fill colours, 189
    changing gradient/bitmap fill
        colours, 190
    closing, 171
    combining, 68
    fitting text to, 91
    resizing, 59
skewed shadows, 174
slideshows (PDF), 216
snapping objects, 55
solid colours, 127, 186, 189
solid transparency, 199
sound, 242
    adding to Web page, 242
special effects, 172, 175
Spell Checker, 119
spelling aids, 118, 119
Split Curves, 69
spreadsheet functions, 129
stacking order, 61
standalone text, 85
star, 170
Startup Wizard, 19, 20
sticky guides, 44
story text, 76
    flowing in frame sequence, 76,
        81
Straight Line Tool, 164, 165
Style Attributes Editor, 183

styles, 181
    object, 181
    setting font, 97
    synchronizing (books), 139
    text, 104
        assigning numbers to, 115
        named, 105
        previewing, 105
        reapply, 108
subscripts, 116
substituting fonts, 100
superscripts, 116
Swatches tab, 167, 190, 191
switching
    between publication windows,
        23
symbols, 115
tab stops, 95
table of contents, 135
    creating, 140
    for PDF file, 214
Table Tool, 123
tables
    Autofit to row/column cell
        contents, 126
    calendars, 130
    distribute rows/columns evenly
        in, 125
    formatting numbers, 129
    inserting formulas, 129
    manipulating, 123
    overview, 122
    QuickClear and QuickFill, 128
    set row height/column width in,
        125
    sorting text in, 124
templates
    design, 20
    logo, 87
text, 75
    adding, to text frame, 79
    applying fonts to, 98
    artistic (standalone), 85
    AutoCorrect and AutoSpell, 118

changing colour or shading of, 189
copying, pasting, moving, 93
default properties of, 25
editing on the page, 92
Find & Replace, 96
fitting to frames, 81
fitting to path, 92
formatting in PagePlus, 97
frames, 75
importing from file, 75, 105
in Web publications, 239
inserting date/time, 116
inserting symbols, 115
inserting user details, 116
on a path, 90
selecting, 92
setting default properties, 25
setting indents, 94
setting tab stops, 95
special effects, 172, 175
table (overview), 122
using gradient and bitmap fills on, 86, 190
Text context toolbar, 97
text frames
creating, 78
linking/unlinking, 83
setting default properties, 24
Text Manager, 81
Text Style Palette, 104
text styles, 104
remove formatting, 107
replace common, 109
synchronizing (books), 139
text wrap, 109
Thesaurus, 121
thumbnails (in printing), 206
tiling (in printing), 207
time field, 116
Timmed Page Mode, 205
tinting, 190
Tool
Artistic Text, 86
Connection Point, 185

Connector, 184
Elbow Connector, 184
Fill, 191
Irregular Crop, 65
Path Text, 91
Pen, 164
Pencil, 164
Pointer, 53
QuickShape, 170
Rotate, 53, 64
Shadow, 174
Square Crop, 65
Straight Line, 164
Table, 123
Transparency, 199, 200
Warp, 178
Transform tab, 59
transparency, 199
applying, 200
Transparency effect, 177
Transparency tab, 199, 200
Transparency Tool, 199, 200
triangle, 170
TWAIN (camera/scanner) source, 158
typeface, 97
Unicode text, 95, 116
unlinking text frames, 84
Update Object Default, 25
Update Text Default, 25
user details, 116
vector images, 147
vertical alignment, 97
video, 242
adding to Web page, 242
view options, 33
warping objects, 178
WAV (Web multimedia), 242
Web colours, 239
Web Publishing mode, 235
Web sites
adding animation effects, 241
adding Java applets, 243
adding sound and video, 242
choosing Web site colours, 238

creating hyperlinks in, 70
getting started, 235
image settings (overview), 240
maintaining, 247
previewing in Web browser,
  244
publishing to local folder, 244
publishing to Web, 245
setting page and file properties,
  241
viewing hyperlinks in, 236
working with hotspots, 236
Welcome to PagePlus X3, 3

What's New?, 3
WMF images, 147
word processor files, 75
workspace
  profiles, 19
wrap outline, 110
  cropping object to, 67
wrapping text around objects, 110
WritePlus, 79
zero point, 45
Zoom Blur effect, 172
zoom view options, 33

creating hyperlinks, 270
deleting, saved, 275
Index, online hypertext II, 240
manifest, 247
previewing in Web browser,
242

publishing locally, fields, 264
publishing to Web, 36
setting, ebook and file properties,
234
version by versions id, 250
working with hotspots, 210
Repeated to InterFlas XS, 3

Wrap Lines, 8
Wrap margins, 147
word processor files, 25
word space
profiles, 19
re-wrap orphans, 140
cropping pictures, 67
wrapping text around objects, 110
WritePlus, 79
auto point, 65
Zoom Blur effect, 127
Zoom View options, 95